T0147500

Heaven On Our Side!

Heaven On Our Side!

Believe In It & It Will Take You There!

**A lost soul who finds herself and
all she can become through the Psychic Medium
Awareness**

Glenda Ann Abell

iUniverse, Inc.
Bloomington

Heaven On Our Side!
Believe In It & It Will Take You There!

iUniverse books may be ordered through booksellers or by contacting:

iUniverse
1663 Liberty Drive
Bloomington, IN 47403
www.iuniverse.com
1-800-Authors (1-800-288-4677)

ISBN: 978-1-4620-2670-8 (sc)
ISBN: 978-1-4620-2669-2 (ebook)

Printed in the United States of America

iUniverse rev. date: 6/7/2011

In Memory Of:

Martin, Joe, Jimmy, Baby Girl, All Our Loved Ones on the Other Side, Laddie Boy, Precious Pup, and All The Spirit and Pet Spirit Loved Ones Who Came Through In The Readings.

I dedicate this book to James Van Praagh, World Renowned Medium, Best Selling Author, and Co-Executive Producer of CBS's Number One Drama Ghost Whisperer. I wish to thank you, James, for showing me to and guiding me through the psychic medium awareness. It was your books, movies, and CD'S that taught me how to tune in the gifts I have. May God Bless You with all that is good. You are my hero and mentor.

Love and Blessings,
Glenda Ann Abell

For those who believe,
No proof is necessary.
For those who do not believe,
No proof is possible.
~ Author Unknown ~

TABLE OF CONTENTS

INTRODUCTION

This is a book of stories that will tell you about my journey into the psychic medium awareness and how it came about. As I tell my stories, I will also be speaking of others that inspired me along the way and gave me the courage to continue on my path of the psychic medium studies. These same wonderful people are still in my life and will be mentioned time and again in my other books. They continue to help me through the good times and the bad.

I was a fifty-year old woman who hated and feared everything. I was a recovering alcoholic of thirteen years. I had been married and divorced three times. I had failed at being a mother, mother-in-law, grandmother, daughter, aunt, and sister. My life still was in total turmoil. I had low self-esteem, felt worthless, and had lived a life of abuse. The abuse was not only from others but also from me to me. After thirteen years of sobriety, I felt my life was no better than when I was drunk. I felt useless and had even contemplated suicide again. That is until the day I went to see a well-known medium at one of his Seminars in Virginia. That day changed my life forever.

My journey through the psychic medium study was not easy at all. There were many times I wanted to walk away from it all but I somehow would be drawn right back. It was the intent and desire of wanting this that kept me going. I wanted to learn and to give to others. I wanted to teach them what so many others along the way had given to me. I was given a second chance and a new way of life.

There were no Psychic Medium Awareness Spiritualist Churches, Development Groups, or anyone else studying the psychic medium awareness locally around me, to my knowledge, at the beginning of my journey. I read, studied, and practiced a well known professional medium's materials to learn from, including his books, television shows, movies, CD's, tapes, website, resource page, chat logs, and interviews to gain more knowledge about the psychic medium awareness. Then, I ventured into other spiritual circles online, participated in chats, read other books, and learned from others. I studied anything that had to do with the psychic medium awareness.

Many people that had known me all my life could not believe I was a medium. There were so many around me at the time that did not believe in psychic medium awareness. I was taught that we are all psychic to some degree. Today, I teach this also. I hope my story will inspire others to search and find their true self as I have done and to learn exactly all they can become. I was told from the beginning in Alcoholics Anonymous that I had to get to the bottom in order to be willing to get sober and stay sober.

In a detailed reading from Alison Baughman, Visible by Numbers, she tells and explains in a life chart number reading, how each step of my life went. Not only from my past, in between, and present, but how my life would unfold in the future. Alison even told me in my phone reading, how I would be moving forward. So far, everything that was said has been totally accurate. Still today, I am living what she predicted.

Alison also told me, "that I had to experience everything I did to be able to help and teach others." This reminds me of what my Father always said, "You have to walk in another man/woman's shoes to truly know him/her." I had to experience losses, struggles, and trials to be able to help others work through theirs. I guess we could say I was to learn compassion, empathy, and unconditional love.

In the stories that follow, it may seem I am scattered. It was recommended to me to be more organized in my stories. However, the way it happened was all scattered, confusing, and sometimes scary. I wrote what came to me in the order that it came to me. I hope the ones who read this book will keep in mind that I am not the most educated person. This is my fault I know. I am hopeful that all who read this book will find inspiration and insight, rather than focus on my writing ability and mistakes in the book.

I start off my book with, "The Fatal Plane Crash", the prologue, for that was when I first started seeking answers to what happened to me that night. Join me in my journey and see how I found the answer I had been searching to find for years.

Namaste - May the Divinity in you find the Divinity in me! May the Divinity in me find the Divinity in you!

PROLOGUE

I was remarried to my ex-husband for the second time, when this experience happened to me. Around this time, I realized that nothing had changed from our first marriage to each other. I was depressed and had low self esteem. I had sold my trailer home and given away most of my belongings when we remarried. Now, I realized our second marriage wasn't working.

I had fallen asleep. My husband always left the television on. The volume had gone up loud and I woke up in a foggy state of mind just long enough to hear that the plane of one of the most famous young men in history went down and he was missing. They weren't sure if anyone else was with him. I remember thinking to myself, "If I could find him, then I would be somebody." I never did become fully awake and fell back to sleep. I found myself on Martha Vineyards. I could see this young man at a distance. It was dark but I knew this man was famous. I couldn't figure out why I was there or how I had gotten there with him. Everything was happening so fast. It was almost like a flash of lightning. The next thing I know, I was walking behind him on the beach. I continued to follow him and watched where he was going. He seemed to be searching for something. While still in my sleep and although I was there with this man, I did not remember what I had heard on the news. I for some reason didn't even resonate with this at the time. I still couldn't figure out how I got there or why I was there.

In the next flash of an instant, I am sitting in an airplane. There was a white light around me the entire time. The light was like a glow and that is how I could see things. The plane was in the ocean. I could see lots of rocks and seaweed through the window. The seaweed was swaying back and forth in the water. Sitting next to me, was this young man. He was white as a ghost. That is the only way I could explain it.

I knew there were two young women sitting in the back seat. My thought was that the one sitting right behind him is his wife. I wasn't sure who the other young woman was. I thought this was the wife's sister or best friend like sister. They were shaking severely and very scared just like me. I said to the young man, "Why aren't you trying to get out of the plane?" I was scared to death for him. "Try at least try, won't you?" There was no reply at first. I said, "Please try to get out of here." He said, "I am at peace now. I am with my mom and dad." I am there trying to understand all this, when he said, "You can go with me, you know." I thought about this for a second. I was trying to figure out what he meant by that. I even tried to see where he was talking about going with him to. My next thoughts were, "No, I have a husband. I am going back home. I am going to try to make my marriage work and then I am going to try to find a job." The young women in the back were still shivering and shaking. I then thought, "I have to get out of here or I am going to die." The woman sitting next to his wife grabbed my arm and said "Please don't leave us here." I just jerked my arm free. I felt myself going through the front window of the plane. I next see myself in a tunnel. It was a very dark tunnel. I could see there was a light at the end of the tunnel behind me. There was a white glow light around me still and this is the only way that I could see where I was at and where I was going. I was soaking wet. I was dripping water everywhere as I walked. My hair was wet and seaweed was hanging all over me. I thought to myself, "I have to get back home and take a shower before my husband realizes I was gone."

At this time, I was heading forward and was three-fourths the way through the tunnel. I continued to walk another few steps through the tunnel and the next thing I know, I was completely dry. The next thing that happened was I felt the bed shaking. It shook so hard, it woke my husband and me. He turned the television off and I slept the rest of the night. I don't recall having any more dreams this night.

I had been going to a hypnotist around this same time to quit smoking. I also saw this hypnotist, when my husband and I had separated previously. I have often wondered if going to the hypnotist opened the doors to what happened this night of my life. I still ask myself that question to this day. I have known some hypnotists since then, that are Mediums, yet I have never asked them if this could have attributed to what happened that night.

The next morning, I jumped out of bed groggily and thought, "I dreamed that the plane of this young man had crashed." My next thoughts were, "I need to work on my marriage and get a job." I had forgotten all about what had happened until around lunch time when my daughter called and asked, "Mom, Have you watched the news?" I said, "No." She then tells me this plane went down with this famous young man on it but they hadn't found it. It was thought after what seemed a long time that the young man's wife and her sister were also with him on the plane.

Slowly but surely, my memory of what had happened the night before came back to me. As I recalled what had happened the night before, I started shaking. I couldn't understand what was going on or what had happened to me. I found myself scared to death. I felt sick to my stomach and was so tired and weary all day.

Over the next few days, as I watched the news constantly, this is what happened. One time I fell asleep on the couch while watching the news. It was after they had found the plane. I was in a big warehouse. I was at the top of the ceiling and looking down. I knew I was where they were investigating and putting the plane back together. There were so many people all around the place. I thought, "I had better get out of here before they see me."

In the next dream that I had, I was watching his famous Senator Uncle. I don't know how I knew it but I knew they were cremating the young man. I saw the famous Senator coming out of this building. In the days to come, the news brought out the fact that the bodies of the famous young man, his wife, and her sister were cremated. I continued to watch everything I could about this matter. I never had any more dreams about this after that; none that I can remember anyway. With all this information that the news was validating and what I had previously seen, I still didn't understand what was happening. It still scared me to death.

I told the story to a few family members. I was afraid to talk about it. I didn't want anyone thinking I was crazy. I couldn't actually talk about something I didn't understand myself.

I made an appointment with my hypnotist. I told him my story as it had happened. I said, "I want you to hypnotize me and take me back there. I want you to know I am telling the truth. I would like for you to help me understand exactly what had happened to me. I don't want you to take me all the way back to inside the plane though because I am afraid if I go back there I will die." I told the hypnotist, "I am afraid I would not be able to get out of the plane and would die this time."

My hypnotist told me, "This is what we call a false dream." He said, "I could take you back there again and that it may be just like you said, but it was what they call a false dream." I looked at him in disbelief. I said, "No, I was there." When the hypnotist said that, I was furious. I did not say anything at all to him. I was furious; I knew this was no fake dream. I knew I was there. I never went back to him again.

SEARCHING FOR ANSWERS

I was still scared over all this. When I thought about it, I would start shaking and feel sick to my stomach again. The fear all came back to me over and over again.

A few weeks later I said, "I know who to talk to. I will call Richard H." Richard H. is my Alcoholics Anonymous Sponsor. Richard H. had told me about several weird things that had happened to him. He had a near death experience (NDE) several times. I didn't know what a NDE was at the time. He just said he died and went through a tunnel. He then told me he came back to life afterwards. The tunnel is what stayed in my thoughts. I too had gone through a tunnel.

Richard H. also talked about his sister everyone called batty. He said she was a psychic and a very good one. I had no clue what he was talking about. I just wanted to know what happened to me.

Richard talked to me a lot about a man named Edgar Cayce. He suggested that I go to the library and find all the books on Edgar Cayce that I could. I did just what he told me to do. I went to the library and spent a lot of time looking through the paranormal section. I had no idea what I was looking for but I brought about twelve books home with me. I went through all the books but I still did not find any answers.

The Famous Medium

Iended up getting divorced again. I continued to work and do the best I could. In time, I had let go of my experience with the fatal plane crash but I never forgot about it. I just tried not to dwell on it. I didn't want all that fear to come back to me.

There used to be an older gentleman that came into where I worked. He used to talk about some strange things. He came in one day and brought me some real old books. He had found them at a used book store. Several of the books he gave me were about Edgar Cayce. I read those books and became a member at Edgar Cayce's A.R.E

This part of my journey was when my family and I watched two famous mediums that had shows on television. I couldn't wait to see these shows come on. I was fascinated by all this. I received a monthly magazine from the A.R.E and on the front page was one of those famous mediums. I couldn't believe what I was seeing. I had to see this medium. I had to see if he could do all those things he said he could do. He talked to dead people. I was skeptical. I didn't know what to think about it.

I made it to his event in Virginia. I was sitting all the way in the back of the room. He asked if anyone had any questions. I have a fear of public speaking but I just knew I needed to ask him a question. I raised my hand hoping he didn't see me. He called on me. I never could understand how he even saw me. I told him about my experience but didn't give the name of the famous person. I just said it was at a famous person's accident. I explained how I had asked my Alcoholic Anonymous Sponsor about the experience and that he told me to read every one of the books I could find on Edgar Cayce. Everyone in the room clapped. I was really embarrassed now. When the medium responded to my question, I never heard him. I don't know what happened for my mind went blank. There was a white like cloud all around me. The medium then puts us all in a meditation. He said, "See in your stomach area two people that have hurt you the most." I saw them plain as day. He says, "Tell them that you forgive them." I did as he said. They were wrapped in white light and they appeared in my stomach area.

As he led us through the meditation, I was crying and could not stop. The more I cried I could see a gold light go from the top of my head to the bottom of my feet. This gold light reminded me of a water cooler bottle. Every time you take a glass of water out of it, you could see the waterline go down further.

He then said, "Look above your head and see in a divine white light, you're passed over loved ones." I did as he said. I could see my father, two brothers, and my baby sister who had been a miscarriage. My mother had a miscarriage about thirty years prior to this event. I didn't and still don't know why my baby sister appeared to me as a five year old. I have doubted many things during my journey. However, I have never doubted that was my baby sister.

The medium brought us out of our meditation. I was in an ozone like state. Ozone state was like being hypnotized. I didn't know what was going on. He then had us do some exercises. One of those exercises was to take a personal item from someone sitting next to you and tell them what you felt or picked up on while holding the object. I didn't have much to say.

THE READING,
THE BEAUTIFUL LADY

During the exercise, a beautiful lady had taken my watch. She had moved her chair right in front of me. She then asked, "Do you smoke?" "I said, "Yes, I do." I said, "Why did you hear me say that outside." She said, "No." She then says to me, "You need to quit smoking."

This doesn't make sense unless you know the entire story here. All the day before and even after I got there, I kept getting thoughts saying this, "I don't want to call on Daddy, Joe, Jimmy, and Baby Girl because they will tell me to quit smoking." I must have thought those thoughts a hundred times before this moment.

All of this went over my head. I did not pick up on what was happening until much later. When I later realized the beautiful lady was a medium and she was giving me a reading, all I could do was cry. Her telling me "You should quit smoking" was the proof my loved ones in spirit were there with me and the medium was real. I cried every time I got alone and thought about the reading.

YOU BROUGHT US TO YOU THERE

One day, two weeks after the event, I was sitting at the kitchen table crying over the reading. I kept getting the thoughts, "You brought us to you there and you can bring us to you here." I heard this about six times. Talking out loud I said, "How?" In thought I heard, "With his VHS tape." I said, "No that doesn't work. I have already tried that."

I had this famous mediums first book, several of his cassette tapes, and a VHS tape that taught you how to do what he did. I had reread his book before going to his event. I had also done the VHS Tape exercises. The one thing I had forgotten to do is close down my chakras properly when I was finished. Chakras are energy centers you open to connect with Spirit. I didn't think it worked because I didn't have some boom bang zip experience. I just didn't know what I was looking for though.

My spirit loved ones had said, "You brought us to you there and you can bring us to you here." Unlike myself I went in and did what I was hearing. I put the VHS tape in and did the exercises. I then put one of his cassette tapes in. They were right. I brought them back to me just like I did at the event.

I practiced meditations twice a day. I brought my spirit family back to me each time. Sometimes other family members and friends would come through and other times strangers would. I didn't say much at first because I wasn't sure if I was imagining things or not. However, it brought a new comfort to me.

I went to the chat site of the famous medium. I read and studied all I could. I practiced my meditations. I eventually had all of the famous mediums resource materials. I couldn't study enough. The more I studied and practiced, the more that would happen. The whole time this was happening to me, my beliefs regardless of what happened was, only certain people could do this; only certain people have "The Gift." I thought only certain people, like the famous medium, had this gift.

MEDITATIONS

The online chat site had a chat room. I crawled in there scared to death. I had never been in a chat room and didn't really know much about it. After I became familiar with this, I found myself going in to chat quite often. I found out that they had meditations twice a week. I just couldn't wait. I loved the meditations.

Bjean was leading meditations on this day. She led us through a meditation to meet up with our loved ones. She said, "See a vehicle of your choosing to come and pick you up." There was my brother Joe. He was in his car that he was killed in. I said, "No Joe, I don't want to go there. I don't want to see that." Somehow I knew Joe was going to take me to the scene of the night he was killed in a car wreck.

I started shaking and I was scared. I then hear a God like voice say, "DO NOT JUDGE WHAT YOU GET." When I say God like voice, it is hard to explain. It comes from above and it is a strong voice. It is loud in a thought type of a voice and it is powerful. I would become familiar with that God like voice as time goes on. I have heard it often. I go and get into the car with Joe. I was sitting in the passenger seat and Joe was driving. Joe showed me what happened. It was at night and dark. I could smell the blood. I had asked, "Joe, are you alright?" Then I thought, "What a stupid question for you to ask. You know Joe died in that car wreck." Just as I had thought that thought, the next thing I know Joe and I were standing in the beauty of nature. That was where we started from before getting in the car. It was daylight again just like when we started. At the scene of the accident, it had been nighttime. We smiled at each other. He had his arm around me and we were walking back the same way which Bjean had taken us. Bjean brought us back to our seats behind the computer. Bjean always asked us to share what we had experienced. Bjean asked me if I experienced anything. I was crying so hard and I told her so. I said, "Bjean, it is too graphic. I don't know if I should." I was still crying. I was crying and couldn't stop. Everyone in the room said, "We are here for you and will help you the best that we can." I told the room what I saw, felt, smelled and heard. They all helped me calm down. Then I felt better.

I won't go into detail about exactly what I saw but what I saw was theorized at the time of the accident. Even the insurance company investigator theorized this but it never could be proven. I did share it with my family. I let go and God knows the truth. I had forgotten until after I had gotten off the computer that recently I had thought the thought, "Maybe one day Joe will show me what exactly happened that night that he died." Today, I know Joe was trying to tell me that he would show me what exactly happened and he showed me.

THE CONTINUED JOURNEY

I continued to go to the meditations. I often thought that what I was experiencing was only in my imagination. However, I still studied as much as I could. I went to the chat room often and shared my experiences. Each time something new would happen, I would share it. I found the message board and shared. I asked questions. I talked about anything and everything. I talked about my past, what I was experiencing then, and what my goals were in the future.

I wanted everyone to be able to see how the study of the psychic medium awareness changed my life. I really didn't care what others thought when they read my posts. If I could help just one person, then all of it was worth it. Once I was told, "You gave too much of yourself." I told about much that happened in my life. I know I am not the only one out there. I wanted others to know that no matter the past they are much more than the human body. We are Spiritual Beings. In the beginning, a lot was ego. Today, I just want to help others.

I started having dreams. The dreams were very vivid. I

didn't know until later these were dream visions. One day I was in the chat room and someone came in named Chuck. The Ops (Chat Room Operators) told me later that he was a medium. He had asked me, "Are you a medium?" I said, "No, I am nobody. I just talk to my spirit loved ones."

The man named Chuck became a very important and inspirational part of my journey. I looked in one of the books to learn more about what the famous medium called gifts. I read it and reread it. It told you in the book about how one may have one or two of the gifts. It didn't say anything about one having all the gifts.

It seemed to me like everything was happening so fast. Like someone or something had pushed a fast forward button. I was hearing spirit, seeing spirit, feeling spirit, and having Dream and Psychic Visions. I would no sooner wonder about something or think about something and it would happen.

GUIDES AND ANGELS

I continued to go to the chat room. I read all I could read. I continued to study and practice. I continued to search for a local development group. I was always wishing to take a professional class. Things were happening fast. At least I now knew I wasn't crazy. One of the family chatters told me that I was a medium. I only thought the famous ones on television could do this. It wasn't until much later I learned that we all are psychic to a degree. We all have the gifts. It depends on if you wish to tune it in or not. I continued to look forward to meditation time at the Meditation Chat Room with Bjean and all the other Ops.

When I was alone at home doing meditations, I would tune into spirit communication with the same meditation cassette tape each time. One time I wanted to tune into communication. I put in the cassette tape and it wouldn't work. I said, "Oh no, I will have to order another one." No matter what I tried I couldn't get it to play. The thought came to use the famous medium's VHS tape. I put the VHS tape in instead. I can't help but to smile here, for after the meditation session the cassette tape worked fine. Communication with my guides, loved ones, and spirit was so good they were directing me to what to use, books I needed to read, and what I needed at the time.

I tried to do my meditations consistently around the same time everyday as was recommended in the resource materials so spirit would know when to be there. I also read that spirits have agendas too.

*Note; Some Teachers believe that Angels and Guides are one in the same. I believe it is what you feel they are, Angels or Guides.

Dream Visions

I started having dream visions more frequently and they were more vivid. One time I was on another level in my dream: It was like I was in Heaven. I was talking to my brother Joe. Joe was showing me that one of my best friends that had passed was with him. She was there in this dream as well. Joe says, "Glenda you have to go back now. You have to get up and get ready to go to work." I said, "No Joe, I want to stay longer."

The next thing I know the phone was ringing. I finally woke up enough to answer the phone. The man on the phone asks, "Is Joseph Abell there?" I smiled for I new what was happening. I said, "No he isn't: May I take a message?" The man said, "No Thank You! I will call at another time."

I was afraid to tell the man on the phone the truth. I didn't want to say, "Joseph Abell is in Heaven." I felt if I did, Joe would never call me back again. That happened a lot after that, my brother Joe calling me. No one believed me though. I had lived in the same place and had the same number for six years. Never had anyone called asking that question.

One day I had company and it was getting real close to my meditation time. The phone rings and the man asked, "Is Joseph Abell there?" I said, "No he isn't. May I take a message?" The man then says, "Sorry to have bothered you at an inconvenient time. I will call at another time." Joe knew I had company and that is why he said that.

My company looked at me stunned and got up. He said, "Well I guess I had better go." My company thought I was referring to a boyfriend. My company left about ten minutes prior to my standard meditation time. I hadn't mentioned what was happening in my life to that particular person at the time.

I centered myself and did my meditation. I kept hearing that Joe, my brother, was my Gate Keeper. I didn't really know what this meant. I told my family, "Joe is my Gatekeeper and keeps me safe and negative energies away." They still all thought I had gone over the deep end.

The Psychic Medium Awareness

I was studying this and working very hard at night. I was trying to work my way up to taking care of myself. I liked living alone. I didn't want to live with anyone just to be able to make a go of it.

One night I didn't have any money, had no gas in my car, and had no cigarettes. I fell asleep crying because I knew I had to go to work. I asked, "Joe what am I going to do?" I finally fell asleep. The phone rang and woke me up. It was a few minutes before the alarm clock was going to wake me up. I needed to get ready for work. It was my daughter. She asks, "Mom do you have money for gas?" I said, "No." She asked, If I had lunch money." I said, "No." She brought me something to eat, cigarettes, and then took me to fill my car up with gas.

I knew in my heart that Joe had put that thought in my daughter's mind. I just closed my eyes and said, "Thank You Joe." I went on and went to work.

At the time, I only told a couple people in my family about what was happening. They all still thought I was way out in left field, so to speak. My youngest brother would say, "This is my crazy psychic sister, Glenda" Other times he would say, "Don't mind Glenda, she isn't crazy; she just isn't all there." He meant it in love and jokingly. Everyone was worried about me.

Practicing and Learning

The famous medium's site that I would go to had different well-known mediums come to the Events Chat Room. I was always hoping to get one of the readings. I used to pray for a reading. I never did get a reading from there. I did have a lot of my questions answered. Something the mediums would say would help me understand what was happening to me. I would learn from the readings being given to others. I learned a lot from chat logs on the site about many different things from professionals who had given previous chat events.

I had two co-workers at the time that let me talk to them about this. They believed in the psychic medium awareness. They would even let me practice read for them. The rest of my co-workers started making fun of me. They talked bad about me behind my back. We started keeping it hush at work and just not talking about it openly anymore.

My sister-in-law and her mother always let me practice with them doing the readings. I was giving them readings and didn't even realize what I was doing. I just thought I was talking to them.

I often still doubted what I was doing. I had to learn to trust. So many along this journey told me that I needed to trust what I get. I still to this day often don't trust what I get. I am working harder on learning to trust.

Spirit often reminded me of what they told me years before I even knew about the psychic medium awareness, "You have Heaven On Your Side! Believe In It & It Will Take You There." I had no idea at this time, what this all would truly mean someday.

THE UNDERPRIVILEGED ONE

Years prior to my finding out about the psychic medium awareness, there was an actual first degree murder case in our town. The man was convicted of first degree murder. He was sentenced to life plus twenty-two years in prison. His family spent an estimated sixty-thousand dollars on different lawyers to get the man a new trial. The family knew that something wasn't right with the case. The family really wanted the new lawyers to prove that the original lawyer was incompetent. The new lawyers said this was hard to prove and opted to go other routes to obtain a new trial for this man.

It was time for my meditation. This time, before I started to meditate, the thought had come to me to do a practice reading. My next thought was that I didn't know who to practice with as I was at home by myself. Then, I remembered the famous medium had said in one of his tapes to practice with an object or picture. I had a picture of this man so I took the picture and sat it on my coffee table.

I began to meditate while looking at his picture and did a picture reading.

That actual reading would haunt me for years to come. The information that I picked up on in the reading was that the man was innocent of the crime in which he was charged with and convicted of. Night after night that followed, I would have dream visions of what really happened. I was told from spirit that the truth could not be seen from the earth world. What spirit meant was that they could see the truth but it was not the same as what the police and people surrounding the case saw.

In the years to come, the original lawyer in this case was disbarred. He was found guilty of stealing approximately two hundred thousand dollars of a deceased client's estate.

The lawyer allegedly started stealing the money around the same time he was representing the man who would later be charged with and convicted of first degree murder. My thoughts on this are, the man convicted of murder doesn't need a psychic to show this lawyer was incompetent. Common sense can tell you that if the lawyer was disbarred for something that allegedly occurred during the time he was representing this man, he was not of legal competence to be representing the man and that showed throughout the trial.

Over and over again, before I ever knew about the psychic medium awareness, I kept hearing during and after this man's trial, "Heaven On His Side! Believe In It & It Will Take You There"! Spirit put those thoughts in my head. I again tell you, I had no clue of the psychic medium awareness at the time. Today, I know spirit was talking to me. What spirit meant was that he had to believe that he had Heaven On His Side, he needed to Believe In It and It Would Take Him to the truth that would set him free.

I did not know then what this would truly mean to me in my life and in the future. Many times from this day and during my journey, I would repeatedly hear the words, Heaven On Our Side! Believe In It & It Will Take You There! This I said before.

*The reason I call this story, "The Underprivileged One" is because I heard this man say, "If ever there is a book written about my case, I want the title to be The Underprivileged One."

THE BOSS

I was tired and sleeping soundly when a spirit's face appeared to me. The spirit was "The Boss", a man I had worked for in the past. The Boss had passed to the other side a few years before. Spirit said, "He Didn't Do It." I knew who he was referring to when he said that. It was in reference to a man I worked with when I worked for the Boss.

I woke up shaking as I sat on the side of the bed. I shook my head and said, "No Boss. He isn't in jail." I then told Boss, that the man I spoke of previously was in jail. Both, Boss and the co-worker knew the man in jail.

I dismissed what had happened and went on about my day. Several days later I received a phone call from my ex co-worker's sister, which happened to be one of my best friends. She was crying uncontrollably and told me they had arrested her brother for first degree murder. I spoke with her for awhile and tried to calm her. We agreed to meet with each other and talk.

It wasn't until I was driving to work after her phone call that I remembered the dream I had two days before.

When I pulled into the parking lot at work, I called her back and told her about my dream. I also tried to explain to her what was happening to me since I had seen the famous medium.

I held fast to the belief of what spirit had told me in this case as I had in the prior case. Spirit showed me in dream visions and in meditation what had happened. This man they showed me did not commit the crime he was charged with.

*These two stories were a big part of my desire and intent to go on and learn all I could on the psychic medium awareness. The law does not recognize a psychic's information as evidence. I keep thinking the truth will set them free. In the second case, the man won his appeal for a new trial. The man in the first case is still trying to get a new trial.

TWO LITTLE SPIRITS

I was in another town visiting someone. The lady I was visiting was in the kitchen cooking breakfast for us. I was walking over to the couch in the living room to sit down. I had a cup of coffee in my hand. I stopped so fast that I went forward and almost lost my balance and spilled my coffee. There in front of me in spirit, was a heavyset grandmother like lady with two little girls. They were so clear to me that I didn't want to step on them so I stopped suddenly. I heard, "Child Abuse." I just looked at them and in thought I said, "I am so sorry but I can't help you. I have two cases now that no one believes me about and the police think I am crazy." I told them, "You need to go to the police yourselves and tell them." The three spirits were so real that I thought they were still alive. I was so tired from a lack of sleep and working so late that I didn't realize that they were passed over.

I was working on the computer one day about three months later and was listening to music on the radio when the news came on and told about finding two little girls dead. It was in the town where I had been visiting months earlier. The shocking part was that it was not far from where I was visiting with the lady.

In the months that followed, it came out that there were three sisters. The one was seven years old and still alive. She was locked in a room upstairs in a two story house. She had jumped out of a second story window and ran to a nearby convenience store. The police came and took her to safety. It was then that the little girl told police that she had two sisters. When the police searched the house and found the other two sisters dead.

I will forever believe that the spirit lady and the two little girl spirits went to the house and helped the surviving sister jump two stories without getting hurt and saw that she got help from the police. To me, the spirits did as I suggested to them when they came to me while visiting my lady friend. How amazing is spirit?

There were other cases like this that came through to me. I just couldn't find anyone to believe me enough or that could use the information to help. I finally had to let go of this part of the psychic medium awareness. Please know that if I could have understood what I was receiving, I would have tried the very best I could to help. In places where the law does not want any help or assistance from a psychic or medium, there is not much anyone can do. Fortunately, in this day and age, a lot of Law Enforcement Agencies are more open to and accepting of help from psychics and mediums. If contacted, I refer clients to well known professional psychic detectives who are specialize specifically in that area.

Alcoholics Anonymous & Psychic Medium Awareness

I had been in Alcoholics Anonymous thirteen years when I went to see the famous medium in Virginia. Just like with studying the psychic medium awareness, I had studied Alcoholics Anonymous. I had read the "Big Book" of Alcoholics Anonymous three times before I had even gone to my first Alcoholics Anonymous (A.A.) meeting. Although Alcoholics Anonymous is based on spirituality, it is not based on any one particular religion. You have a higher power of your choice in Alcoholics Anonymous.

Nowhere, did I read the writer of the "big book" was a medium but I personally believe he was a medium based on his burning bush spiritual experience and other incidents. In layman terms, he had seen the light. No doctors or priests could help him to stop drinking. His belief in this new found spiritualism is the only thing that could help him quit drinking. I also feel the "Big Book" was written inspirationally. Inspirational Writing is when someone in the Spirit Realm helps you by guiding you what to write about. Some also call it auto-writing or channeling.

I could probably take the Big Book of A.A. and discern it the way I was seeing it when I first started studying the psychic medium awareness. However, I am only going to talk about a few things I picked up on that I feel are similar in both areas.

The big book of A.A. teaches us that we are powerless over people, places, and things. Spiritualism teaches us we have no right to try to control another's path. We must go to any lengths to obtain sobriety. Spiritualism teaches us that it is our intent and desire when tuning in our gifts of the psychic medium awareness. How much do we desire to practice and learn the psychic medium awareness? Once we tune in our gifts what is our intent to do with the gifts? Are we going to help others with our new found gifts? We are taught that A.A. is there to help all; the hand of A.A. is always there and let it begin with me.

One of the principles of A.A teaches, ***Principles before Personalities***, you take what you can use from the meeting and leave the rest. In other words, if you don't like something or someone around the A.A. meeting, you overlook the negative and draw from the positive.

We all learn the psychic medium awareness in our own way. We cannot let other's personalities or disbeliefs interfere with our beliefs in A.A or the psychic medium awareness. Do not judge others. Don't take another's inventory in A.A.

I think what the writer of the Big Book of A.A. had experienced a spiritual experience. To me, he had become aware of the psychic medium awareness. Basically, what we experience when we become open to this the awareness. Just my thoughts on this and this truly amazed me when I started to study the awareness.

A.A. Sponsor Richard H.
&
Alanon Sponsor Gail H.

You may recall what I said earlier, that my A.A. Sponsor was the one who suggested that I go to the library and get all the books I could find on Edgar Cayce. Ironically, the seminar where I went to see the famous medium, was at Edgar Cayce's Foundation at the A.R.E. When I mentioned that at the seminar, everyone in the room clapped when I said that? I smile thinking about it now but at the time I blushed because I had brought their attention to me without realizing it.

Being anonymous is a very important part of A.A. This was a very big part of A.A that I didn't understand until much later on in recovery. My sponsors gave me permission to use their names here. In the psychic medium awareness, the ego has to be left out just the way it has to be left out of your recovery in Alcoholics Anonymous.

When I would ask Richard H., my A.A. Sponsor, certain questions he would always say, "Let me talk to my

Spiritual Advisor." I asked, "What is a Spiritual Advisor?" He chuckled and said, "One day you will find yours." I wanted to know about his. Richard's wife Gail was my Alanon Sponsor. I had relapsed in A.A. so many times that most sponsors just shook their head. However, Richard and Gail never gave up on me. Gail would always say every time I talked to her, "Remember we love you." No matter what I did or said, they always reminded me of the love they had for me. In the psychic medium awareness we are taught to love unconditionally. Richard and Gail have always loved me unconditionally.

I quit school in ninth grade. I got married and had a baby. I didn't get my high school diploma until I had gotten sober in A.A. at the age of thirty-eight. I kept telling Richard, "I don't know if I can do this." Richard always looked at me and chuckled and said "You can do it."

I love that chuckle he gives. He told me, "If you go in there with an attitude that you can't do it, you won't." He told me to change my attitude and keep it positive. Later on, I found that similar to A.A., the psychic medium awareness, teaches us we are Spiritual Beings and have the power within us to do anything we desire. It also teaches us to always keep in positive thoughts and light. I got my diploma. Then, I wanted to learn to type. I went to the basic typing class and learned how to type thirty words a minute. Richard told me I could do that too. He repeated to me the above.

Richard and Gail had what I wanted. They had sobriety and a loving way of life. They are always there for each other and for so many others in A.A. and Alanon. These beautiful people have had their own share of problems: primarily health issues.

Richard was and continues to be my sponsor, although

Glenda Ann Abell

A.A. suggests woman have woman sponsors. When I got sober, there weren't that many sober woman sponsors at the time. Some of the women sponsors they did have, had gone back to drinking and/or doing drugs after a long length of sobriety. Some have even passed away since going back, due to the drinking and/or drugs.

Richard and Gail could write a book of their own about what they have seen, heard, and learned over the years. Although I haven't stayed in touch with them much in these later years, they have always been on my mind, and they have always been there for me whenever I have called upon them. I have to say I love them so dearly.

THE ONES WHO HAVE
INSPIRED ME

In this section, I will be sharing stories of those who have given me their time, love, wisdom, guidance, and support along the way. These people have inspired me with their strength, courage, and enlightenment. There are many of the same people mentioned here still with me in my journey today.

THE BLESSING IN DISGUISE:
MICHAEL & RAPHAELLE TAMURA

I had been to some of the special chat events at the famous medium's website when two of the most world-renowned healers, Michael and Raphaelle Tamura, had events there. At this time, it was still early on in my journey and I didn't really understand about the healing or healers. That comes much later in my journey.

I went back to review their old chat logs and read all the past events they had done. When doing this, I never dreamed of how or what an astronomical part these two wonderful healers would play in my journey. When I hear the word healer, my first thoughts are of these two.

At this one site, they also had a prayer circle event in one of the chat rooms. I had only attended it maybe two times. The second time I went was wonderful. It was a warm and comfortable feeling in the prayer room.

A woman came in whom I knew and had chatted with many times. We had emailed back and forth. We had laughed together and cried together. I sensed she was hurting deeply.

It was close to the anniversary of her son's passing and she was requesting prayers. The feeling of pain stayed with me. I had closed down the computer. I had the thought in my mind, "When I learn how to read for people I am going to read for her." I was hoping I could bring a connection to her from her son.

This was what was happening as I have previously said, I could think about wanting to do something with the psychic medium awareness and then boom it would happen. I would soon thereafter experience it.

I was ironing clothes. I had worked the night before. I was really tired. Back then when I washed clothes, I had to iron every single piece of clothing before hanging them up. I even ironed t-shirts. After a couple hours of ironing, I went to take a nap. I was in like a dream state. I call it the twilight zone state or ozone state. I didn't know exactly what I was seeing at the time. I know today what I was seeing in my vision was two well-known mediums giving out readings. The two mediums step back and I am standing there with the young man. The young man was telling me that I could give his mom the message.

The young man comes up to me singing a song that I knew went with the woman who had come to the prayer circle asking for prayers. The young man starts talking to me. He gave me a message to give to his mom. When I woke up, I wrote down what I could remember. I even had his name and his description. I am sure someone mentioned his name before in the chat rooms but I never focused on that and didn't recall his name. I had emailed this young man's mom and told her what had happened. She validated the description and name.

She later emails me back the most devastating email that

I could ever imagine. She called me a want-to-be medium and said that it was my imagination. She said that if she wanted a reading, she would get one from some well known mediums names she mentioned. She had never sent me a picture of her son. I had no clue of what he looked like. This was my very first experience in receiving spirit like this to deliver a message.

I was crushed. I packed up all books, CDS, bibles, any and everything I had on the psychic medium awareness. I was packing up everything in this plastic container and I was even going to put my Master Guide who was Jesus in the plastic container. I just couldn't lift it and put it in the attic but that is where it was going. I had had it with this; there would be no more studying the psychic medium awareness.

I had also talked with the Reverend who in time would be my online teacher for two years in instant message. He had the same carrier as I did so we could chat in instant message on the computer. I told him what I was going to do. He was a medium also. He emails me back and says, "You need healing first. Don't be surprised if you come back to this at a later time." It was the psychic medium studying he was talking about. I really didn't know what he meant when he said I needed healing. I just knew I had enough of all of it.

I was still crying over this the next day, while I was ironing clothes. It was then, that the young man came up and was standing behind me. I didn't have to turn around and look at him. I could see him without turning around. Today, I know the reason I didn't have to turn around to see him was because I was seeing him through my psychic eye. I never did turn around because I could see him the entire conversation.

I just kept crying only harder now and kept right on ironing my clothes. It hurt me deeply to say to this young man spirit what I said to him next. I said, "Go away, you aren't there. You are my imagination and I don't see you. You aren't real and this isn't real." I cried harder all along. The young man tried to talk to me some more. I screamed, "GO AWAY! YOU AREN'T THERE!" I was hoping my neighbors didn't hear me. He put his head down and turned around and walked a couple steps and disappeared. I knew what I had done. I had read everything I could on this and knew that you don't do this to spirit. You try to explain to them why, calmly and nicely. I now know this young man and his mother was a Blessing in Disguise. His mother doesn't know it; I know the spirit young man knows, but this put me with the connection with the two world-renowned healers.

The Reverend Medium from the site said that I needed healing. There was that word again. I was doing a meditation of healing. I was still hurting bad and crying a lot. So, I went to the resource page on the one website. There I found and clicked on Michael Tamura's website. I couldn't believe what I was seeing. He had written an article and its title was "No, It's Not Your Imagination." I couldn't tell you how many times I just stared and read that article over and over again. After that, I took all the materials out of the plastic container and put them back on the bookshelves. I asked my Master Guide to forgive me. I had emailed the healers about everything that happened. Even about how I locked my Master Guide in the box, so to speak, and was putting him in the attic too.

I went into meditation with the famous medium's tape to connect with spirit. I said to the young man spirit, "If you can hear me, please come back and talk to me. I would like to talk to you." The young man spirit came walking up to me. It was like he was in my computer room on my level and close to me. This was unusual because I didn't let spirit get close to me on my level. I had a pact with spirit; for they were to stay on the Heaven's level. I didn't want them to spook me by being close to me. It was the fear I had within me of them being a ghost. However, he didn't spook me at all. I told him how sorry I was for so rudely sending him away. I told him I had been hurt deeply by what happened. He talked to me and we made amends. The young man spirit later appeared quite a few times in the spiritual chat rooms when I was doing practice readings. I never brought him through in reading. I let other readers do that.

A few days later I received an email from Michael Tamura. He recommended that I read his book, "You Are the Answer." At the end of his email he said, "Glenda, by the way I don't think your Master Guide would have stayed in that box or in the attic." I burst out laughing. I guess he was right on that one. Just imagine trying to lock Jesus up in the attic. I hadn't laughed in weeks. I ordered Michael's book as he recommended. I received the book less than a week later and read it. I loved it from the very beginning. After reading his book, I had a sense of knowing his wife Raphaelle.

When I was working on my website, I decided to add links to those professionals who had helped and inspired me in my study of the psychic medium awareness. When I went to add Michael and Raphaelle's link to my website, I got to know Raphaelle even better. She became a very integral part of my spiritual journey. No matter how busy she was, Raphaelle would give me guidance on so much about the psychic medium awareness. She would also share her wisdom and knowledge. I can't help but to smile when I think about her bringing to my attention that I often ran my sentences together. This is very true; I still do it to this day. I will think to myself, "Raphaelle would get me if she saw this email." Meaning she would correct me or remind me what she had taught me about running my sentences together.

During readings, when I would have new experiences, I would write and tell Raphaelle all about it. Raphaelle helped me through another devastating downward spiral. I wanted to give up the mediumship again. Raphaelle emailed me and said, "Glenda, I say this to you with love, hurt feelings are the ego and the ego does not justify you giving up that which will bring healing to many others." After that, I didn't let much of what others said bother me. Right after this downward spiral, I had a group reading to do. I emailed Raphaelle and told her that I had a group reading to do. It was my first in person reading since this downward spiral. I told Raphaelle how nervous I was. Raphelle later emails me and says "G if you don't trust in yourself then trust in spirit." Raphaelle had started calling me G and I liked that.

When I got to where I had to go to do the readings, I was very nervous. I recalled mentally what Raphaelle had said about trusting in spirit. Raphaelle was right. I did the group readings and spirit pulled me through. Everyone was happy with their readings.

Today, I often recommend Michael Tamura's award-winning book "You Are The Answer" to others. Michael's book is an extraordinary guide to entering the sacred dance with life and fulfilling your soul purpose. It was recommended to me by Raphaelle that I use my own words describing Michael's book. My words couldn't give Michael's book enough validation. I even recommended this book to Bjean who has taken dozens of classes and is a Reiki Master, Healer, and Teacher. She thanked me whole heartedly for recommending this book she loved as well.

Later on, I even became a Reiki One. I studied more on the healing powers. Nothing could help teach me how powerful the healing powers truly are as much as Michael Tamura's "You Are The Answer." It helped make me realize and accept that I am a Spiritual Being in a Human Body.

Michael's book taught me how much the material world is not what it seems to be. It taught me how the past does not hold me back from becoming the true Spiritual Being I am. It taught me more of what my life's purpose truly is.

PROFESSIONAL MEDIUM, CHUCK BERGMAN

Chuck Bergman is a Professional Medium I found on the resource page of a website I was going to. He lives in Florida, near my sister. I had looked at the resource page many times and always wanted a reading. I know the family chatter on the Message Board told me I was a medium. I read many times where a medium would talk about how they got a reading from another medium. I couldn't understand that. Why would a medium need a reading from another medium? I learned the answer to that as my journey studying the psychic medium awareness comes about.

I didn't have the money to buy a reading. I called one of my brothers and I asked him for the money. My brother always listened to me. He never passed judgment on me; if he did he didn't say it to me personally. When I first started realizing my gifts and abilities in psychic medium awareness, it showed me that Jesus was my Master Guide. I told this same brother that my Master Guide is Jesus.

He said, "Well I do believe you have one of the best." I get giggling whenever I think about his response.

My brother gave me the money to buy a reading from Psychic Medium Chuck Bergman. Chuck Bergman was a retired policeman. I was so excited I was getting a reading from Chuck Bergman. I had been at one of the Special Events at the chat room and Chuck was the Guest Speaker. Chuck even did a drawing for two people who would win a free reading from him but I didn't win a reading. It didn't matter now though, for I was finally going to get a reading from Chuck.

Chuck gave me a very accurate detailed reading. He brought through my brother Joe. He says, "This is strange, I am seeing a pair of scissors. I have never seen this before in this way. It is like someone is getting a haircut. I picked right up on what Chuck was saying. I said, as I recalled in my mind, what had happened, "Oh My Gosh!" I wanted to start crying. My brother Joe wore his hair long, which was in style at the time of his passing. When I walked up to the casket to see Joe and pay my respects, I was shocked that his hair was short. I can't remember if Joe voluntarily got his hair cut that day or if it was cut after the accident. Joe hadn't worn his hair short like that since he was a young boy. I had forgotten about that until Chuck brought it through in his reading. All of this was validation to me that Chuck was talking to my brother Joe in spirit.

Chuck then says, "Glenda someone is saying you wrote four or five sentences or paragraphs about them." I said, "Yes for Joe." I wanted to put this on a plaque at his grave site,

"Walk Through This World With Me; Go Where I Go, Share All My Dreams With Me, For I Love You So." This was part of the lyrics in one of country music singer

George Jones' songs. I validated this to Chuck. Today, as I look back at this, I would say Joe has walked my journey with me. He is with me as my Gatekeeper now. I never knew back then, the true meaning of those words or the message being given. I would hear that song often in the days following Joe's passing. I now realize, Joe has been and continues walking my path with me. Joe is with me during every reading I give. In the beginning, he was always there when I brought spirit through and still is. Joe's message to me was and is "I will walk through this world with you; I will go where you go, and I will share all your dreams with you, for I love you so."

Chuck mentioned a flight of stairs right after this in his reading. I immediately thought about my sister-in-law's father, whom I had written a eulogy about for and from my brother. Before my sister-in-law's father passed, he told his family members he saw their deceased loved ones waiting for him at the top of the stairs and he was ready to go up the stairs now. He passed just after he said this.

I never validated all this to Chuck. Remember this was my first reading. I honestly didn't know what to expect. I was seeing everything Chuck brought through in his reading to me. I did not realize until much later, this was my psychic medium awareness.

Later on in the reading, I asked Chuck, "What am I?" Chuck asks, "What do you mean, what are you?" I asked, "Why are spirits talking to me?" He said, "You are just like me. You will one day help other people." I told Chuck, "I help people in Alcoholics Anonymous. I lead A.A. meetings." Chuck then said, "No, not like that. You are what I am. You are a medium and one day you will be giving readings just like I do." He goes on to say, "They say you have been in the gutter many times but you are strong and you keep pulling yourself up again. Eventually you will help others to pull themselves up again. You are strong like that, he says again." Well now I was very glad Chuck couldn't see me. I was rolling my eyes. I said to myself in thought, "Here this medium has given me such an awesome detailed accurate reading and he said one day I would be doing what he does." I didn't' believe it for a minute. I couldn't understand how Chuck could do the phone readings. I also couldn't understand how mediums could stand in front of people doing readings like they did. No way was I going to ever be able to do that. Chuck went on with many more details and however accurate, this part of the reading, he was wrong.

Almost two years later, I emailed Chuck. I said, "Chuck, guess what?" I told him what was happening in my world. I asked Chuck if I could give him a practice reading. Psychic Medium Chuck Bergman, as busy of a man as he is said "Yes." I had asked him to send me a picture to focus on. He did. So now, I was going to be doing a reading for Chuck Bergman, a Professional Psychic Medium. I was nervous and concerned that I would blow the reading for Chuck and even asked myself, "What have you gotten yourself into now?"

Just before Chuck was to call for his reading, I needed to do a meditation to connect with spirit to be able to give him his reading. So, I proceed to do the meditation to connect with spirit. In this, I saw Chuck's loved ones sitting on my couch and they knew I was concerned about blowing this reading because they said, "We will help you." I said, "I sure hope so. He is one of the most professional mediums there is." I could feel their love and pride for Chuck coming from them. It was a truly wonderful feeling.

That was only the second time I let spirit get close to me on my level. Remember; I had a pact with spirit; for they were to stay on the Heaven's level. I didn't want them to spook me by being close to me. It was the fear I still had within me of them being a ghost.

Now it was time to give Chuck his reading. Chuck called me for his reading. I told him I was nervous. He was patient with me and validated things that I was seeing, feeling, and hearing in thought and explained how it resonated to him. He explained readings and the process of the mediumship. When I first started describing spirits other than Chuck's family, Chuck validated that these spirits were from readings he had given earlier that day. It scared me to think that Chuck still had a houseful of spirits even though his readings were done.

I had also heard Chuck on Alison Baughman's online radio show where he spoke about his journey to becoming a medium and gave readings afterwards. I attended several chat events on another well-known psychic medium's chat site where Chuck was guest speaker. That is where Chuck brought through my best friend who passed right before my eyes, several hours after he passed. I finally got to meet Chuck in person at one of his events in Jacksonville, Florida where I had a front row seat. Wow! The energies at that event were indescribable. The people there loved him. This overwhelming love was such a wonderful feeling.

What's so amazing to me is that these well-known professionals are not smug or ego based. They are down to earth human beings filled with love and compassion. They go out of their way to help others.

Featherwind & Petz, One With The Light!

I love telling many of my stories but this is one of my favorites. Featherwind & Petz are two of my online teachers. It was their class I went to the most. They taught others how to do online readings at one of the other chat sites. Featherwind would walk us through a short meditation to connect with spirit for the readings. My favorite one was The Energy Ball. The Energy Ball also worked for protection of higher good. It would be a ball of gold divine energy light that we would pass from one to another in the room and see the gold divine universe light that surrounded us. At the end of the line, Featherwind then would tell us to see this gold divine light surround the entire room. This seemed to work best for me. Even when Featherwind would do a different meditation, I would say, "Featherwind, could I please borrow your gold divine energy ball?" She would always say, "Sure you can." Here it is and pass me the ball. Sometimes I would forget to pass it back when done. Featherwind would remind me to give the Energy Ball back. This went on for months. One day I opened an email that was sent to me from Petz. It Read, "Here's Your Own Energy Ball." It was the most beautiful picture of a man holding a ball of light up in the air." I printed that picture out and put it on the top of my computer desk in a frame. I would look at that picture and do meditations with that Energy Ball before doing Readings.

The next time I was in class, I asked Featherwind if I could borrow the Energy Ball. Petz speaks up and says, "No way, you have your own energy ball now." I laugh even now as I write this.

Many times if I had problems or questions I could email Petz and Featherwind. When I was to do my very first in person reading I emailed Petz and said, "Petz, I am nervous." Petz emailed back and said, "Glenda, You are going to love this. It is so much different than online reading. The connection is much easier and clearer." In the stories that follow, I will be telling you about my first in person group reading.

Petz and Featherwind later started calling me by my first name, Glenda, except in the chat rooms where we all basically had made up nicknames. I know Featherwind's first name but not last. I never knew Petz's real name until years later.

I was practicing building websites. Just like everything else, I had no clue of what I was doing. I learned by trial and error. For a long time my first website didn't have much on it. After practicing awhile I just kept learning more. I love Petz and Featherwind so much that I wanted to "Pay It Forward" so to speak. I had never heard anyone mention that Petz and Featherwind had a web site, not even Featherwind or

Petz. So, I decided to build them one. If they didn't like it I would remove it.

Every time I looked at that energy ball my thought was "One With The Light!" I really wanted to call it Featherwind & Petz's. I kept hearing in thought, "One With The Light." I feel spirit helped me name this one. I honestly felt that about all the sites I practiced building. I felt certain spirits gave me the title for them, no matter if the site was for me or someone else. Petz had asked me to dedicate her part of the website to her cousin Oliver, whom had passed. Petz sent me a picture of Oliver. Keep in mind that I was and am still fairly new at this website building. At this time, I had also done some picture readings. I felt Oliver's presence with me while I worked on the site. I even saw Oliver when I wasn't looking at the picture. I thought that was because I had looked at his picture so much. I kept trying to put that picture on there as a large picture. Well I did this about fifty times because half the time it wouldn't take or if it did take, it didn't look right. Somehow Oliver had me click something and the picture became smaller so I added it to the website. It was perfect. To this day, I believe Oliver helped me make the picture look picture perfect.

I remember mentally thanking Oliver. I said, "That does look much better." I even felt a brush on my cheek and then I see what looks like Oliver's spirit kissing me on the cheek out of gratitude. I thought this was my imagination. I had grown very tired. I didn't say anything about all this at first to Petz.

Featherwind wanted her part of the website dedicated to her mom, whom had passed. I felt her mom with me as well the whole time. I had a hard time trying to make Featherwind's mom's picture small. Again, I clicked a button or did something and finally got it right. I still didn't know how I made it smaller. I felt Featherwind's mom helped me. After I had finished building the site, I still didn't know how to make the pictures smaller. I still don't know how to make a picture smaller right today.

One evening, I was working on Petz and Featherwind's site when I felt and saw Oliver again. Again, I thought this was because I had seen his picture so much. Then, I finally realized "I do picture readings so why wouldn't I see spirit." I thought I had to go into meditation to tune into seeing spirit. I learned several years later that I didn't really have to do the meditations to see spirit. Each day was new learning experiences.

Oliver was there and I felt he wanted me to give Petz a reading. I contacted Petz and told her this. Petz, Featherwind, and I set a time and date to meet in a private chat room of theirs. I also invited AngelOp Reader Jessica who was and is one of my closest friends to come with me. I brought Oliver through and Jessica brought Featherwind's mom through. The readings were accurate and detailed. They both were happy with their readings.

AngelOp Reader was what we named the room operators in AngelsLanding Chat Room on my website www.HeavenOnOurSide.net that did readings. Petz also gave a reading that brought through my brother Joe. Joe described to Petz all about one of our relatives here on earth and the issues that were going on in his life. Petz said, "Joe wants you to get the message to this relative, "I am with you." Petz went on to describe how Joe was trying to help our relative here. Joe wanted him to know he is loved and is with him.

I looked at the chat logs that Petz had sent to me with

this reading on it. I copied it and pasted it and printed it out. I mailed the entire log to this relative. I didn't even care if he didn't believe in this. I just wanted to do what Joe suggested.

JESSICA & RAY,
MY ROCK ANGELS

I met Jessica in a practice reading class. They eventually closed down the site we all went to for practice reading classes. After that, Jessica connected with me at my chat room AngelsLanding on my website Heaven On Our Side. There we would do practice reading classes and it was learn as we go. I had nicknamed Jessica my Rock Angel. At one time there were a lot of AngelOps and Practice Readers that came to AngelsLanding. Jessica and I would also go to several other chat rooms and lead practice reading classes.

Ray is Jessica's Fiancé and he too became an AngelOp Reader. He read Tarot Cards. He also was a Reiki Master Teacher and did healing readings. We all just bonded. Jessica & Ray are still my Rock Angels to this day. No matter what happened or what we were doing Jessica stood by me. I feel as close to her as I do my own sisters.

We stay in contact and still do readings for one another.

Jessica did what I always dreamed of doing, she took hands on, in person workshops with the famous medium that I had went to see. She has always been and still is a detailed accurate reader. Ray is the same way with his readings.

THE REVEREND

The Reverend had a website and chat room. When the famous medium's site closed for maintenance, the Reverend taught classes at his chat room. Jessica and I were two of the co-hosts during these classes. I was in the Reverend's chat room talking to him and one of his room operators when the Reverend asked me to connect with his room operator. I said, "Let me go do a meditation first." The Reverend said, "No, you don't need to do anything. Just give what you get." He then proceeded to teach me how to connect with spirit without doing anything.

I first brought the room operator's uncle through. The Reverend said, "Ask Spirit to come closer to you." I was a little afraid at first. I said to Spirit in thought, "Come closer please." The Reverend said, ask Spirit to come closer, ask spirit to come closer still." He did this until I was in spirit's energy or spirit was in mine. The room operator's uncle got so close to me that it felt like a tingle and electric shock at the same time. I said, "ouch and then wow." The Reverend said, "You did very well." The Reverend already knew his room operator's spirit loved one was there and he wanted to see if I could pick that up.

I had been joking around with this. I was sort of caught off guard when the Reverend asked me to do the reading. The Reverend then said, "You must respect spirit. They come a long way to meet with you and to connect with you." Mentally I then tell spirit, "Please come on and sit down by me." Spirit sat down beside me. I said, "Ok, I am ready to go on with the reading. I have asked him to sit down next to me." The Reverend said, "You Did What?" I could sense the Reverend was yelling at me. At least that was what it felt like to me.

The Reverend's mother then appeared. I had read for him once before but became intimidated because of who he was and had to let Bjean take over. We were in someone else's chat room at the time. I still remembered the Reverend's mother from that reading. I said, "Your mother is here and she is shaking her finger at you for being hard like that on me." She says, "Like she was on you." He was coaching me or reprimanding me, I thought. What he was doing was trying to teach me discipline. The Reverend said, "Yes, she was very strict on me." The Reverend went on to tell us more on how strict she was on him. I then said, "Mom says see where it got you?" The Reverend said, "What does that mean?" By this time I felt the Reverend was losing patience with me. His mom then repeated, "See where it got you; you are now a Spiritual Reverend." The Reverend said, "Point well taken."

The Reverend had gone to one of the most famous and strictest Medium Schools in London. He had already discussed the discipline used. So, by my asking spirit to sit next to me, I don't think it was acceptable to him. I know many times others thought I was acting up in class but in all reality I was being me. I wasn't purposely being silly or stupid acting.

The Reverend went on to say, "I only do it because I want the very best for you." I said, "Mom says she only wanted the best for you." I went on and finished the reading. I was so grateful for his mother showing up that day.

Psychic Reading, Mental Telepathy

O ne of my teachers suggested I keep this quiet because many in the chat rooms that just wanted to chat might not care much for this. I could not only feel how they were thinking about me, I sometimes picked up their thoughts about me even on line. At first, I thought it was my own thoughts. This happened even at work, around people and on the phone.

I soon started to be more mindful of this. I had to be careful. I would answer someone's thoughts even when they hadn't openly said what they were thinking. For example, my Mother would call me and she would be thinking something like, "That must be nice." I would say, "Yes that was nice." She hadn't said a word but I knew what she was thinking. This got me in trouble many times.

At work someone could be tired and grouchy around me and even if I wasn't, I would soon become tired and grouchy. I was picking up other's thoughts and energies. I would soon act like them. Several had anger management problems and I would end up screaming like they did. This proved to me thoughts are real and you get back what you give out. I would be negative toward the ones who were that way toward me. I gave them back what they were giving out.

I started using one meditation from the famous medium's book of meditations. The meditation said to see a reversible mirror around you. After you do that, you see a pink light around the reversible mirror. He said that you reflect negative thoughts back to anyone sending you the thoughts, but with loving thoughts attached. I found it worked often when I remembered but many times I would forget. Those times were the times I would act unacceptable. It was too late for I would get angry and be negative.

This happened to me during my last downward spiral. Right after I received negative emails telling me that I was a fake, phony, want-to-be medium with a delusion of grandeur, I was talking to Jessica in instant message online. Jessica said, "See you are being negative toward me" I apologized and said, "Let me go take a sea salt bath." We both laughed about it. I went and took a sea salt bath. Jessica let me do practice readings for her family which she wouldn't have if she didn't believe in me and trust me. We came to realize what was happening. I have often seen it happen to others on line.

If I tried to explain it to them, they would turn on me and say it was just me. I made up my mind not to say anything anymore. Let them learn their own path. I have seen ones that would try to discredit another reader. This has happened to me many times. I caught myself letting it get to me. The saddest part about all this is that I gave so many accurate readings in the chat rooms that I could not believe some of those that turned their backs on me. Then,

I remembered what professionals like Alison Baughman, Chuck Bergman, Shelley Duffy, Raphaelle Tamura, and Jessica said to me in love and support. Those were true professionals so why should I let those who have no idea get me down or upset me.

In Alcoholics Anonymous my Sponsor called this, "Letting others rent space in your head for free." In the Mediumship it was called, "Giving others your power."

My Experiences Along The Way

Now I will talk about some of the other experiences I had along the way of learning more about the psychic medium awareness, reading online, and in person readings. Some of the events are painful or sad. Others are humorous.

Learning more about the psychic medium awareness has helped and continues to help me heal more as time goes on. Still I often become confused and scattered. I've learned that when I get like that, I must go back and center myself. I have to keep the balance in my life. I am sure much of my journey would have been simpler if I had a development group to go to in my local community. Had I had a Professional Psychic Medium Awareness teacher to teach me hands on in-person, I believe it may have been much easier for me to learn and understand but I am a firm believer that everything happens for a reason.

Raphaelle Tamura said to me in an email, "Glenda it may not be so bad, you are learning on your own this way." I felt there was truth and good meaning behind what she was saying. Today, I feel it is to my advantage in the long run because when I teach others, I will have a more first hand knowledge of the experiences. I can also teach better how not to have the negative experiences that I have had. I can better help them work through similar things that they may be experiencing.

FEAR, FAITH, & CODE OF ETHICS

In all that I have studied, you are told about the fear. The famous medium said fear is false evidence appearing real, fear feeds negative energies, and fear snowballs. The more fear you put out the more fear you draw to you along with all the negative energies.

Before my psychic medium studies, fear controlled my life. I was afraid of living, dying, and people. I feared traveling. I was afraid of heights. I also have what I call stage freight. I am afraid of public speaking. I was afraid to go across bridges. I was claustrophobic. I was simply afraid of everything around me.

The more I studied to be a psychic medium, the more I understood how to alleviate much of the fear. Every time I was in a downward spiral, it was based on some type of fear. I am working on replacing the fear with faith. I should have known this based on prior experiences. Every time I was afraid of something, it became overwhelming. If I faced my problems, eventually the answer came. If I find myself becoming fearful, I do everything I have been taught to do to remove the fear. I will do positive affirmations, meditations, and go within to gain my courage back. The main thing I need to do is renew the faith in my life.

You need to know and remember always that nothing I say in this book takes the place of medical or professional help. I am just sharing things that have helped me along the way and hope that they too can help you. I have suffered with depression and anxiety since I was around seventeen.

In my journey, I have found what the famous medium said about not all psychics are spiritual, to be true. I like to think I stick to the code of ethics the best as possible. When I received my very first professional phone reading, a young woman called me asking if I would read for her. She wanted a psychic reading. She was pregnant and when she was sixteen years old a psychic told her when she was nineteen or twenty years old she would get pregnant and have a miscarriage. She was twenty years old and pregnant.

I really didn't give too many psychic readings. I didn't even know if I could give her a psychic reading. I said well I am a psychic medium and I normally just do medium readings. I started seeing spirit and seeing different scenes. I was telling her what I was seeing. Then it showed me children. I saw two children a boy and a girl. I did not feel fear with the birth. After the reading, I suggested that she go by doctor's orders, not to overdo anything, and to not do any heavy lifting. I just told her the everyday common sense things that go with pregnancy. When the reading was over with she said, "How much do I owe you for the reading. I said, "Nothing. If you want you can make a five dollar donation to my site." She said she would but she never did. This happened many times in the future. Someone would want a reading and promised to pay for it and never did. If a person couldn't afford a reading, I would give them one. The ones who paid thousands of dollars over time for readings from other psychic mediums are what bothered me most.

In the beginning, I had a problem with charging for a reading. It was not long ago that I was told that if you worked a regular job you would expect to get paid. I even had one professional tell me that if you don't charge for a reading, they don't think the reading is worth anything.

I was in practice readings at one of the chat rooms one evening. I read for a lady who wanted to know if she should go to the hospital to see her aunt. What she was asking me was if the aunt was going to die. She had to travel quite a ways to get there. I saw the relative that she was talking about in the hospital bed. I saw her loved ones in spirit around her. This was not unusual for me to see. I see loved ones with people all the time at hospitals. I get more of the feeling they are there for moral support. At the end of the reading I said, "Know that at any time, whether it be ten years from now, your relatives in spirit that I just described will be there to help her cross over."

I never saw this woman in the chat room again until about eight months later. She comes in and says, "I am looking for Glenda." Someone in the room waiting for a reading said, "Everyone's looking for Glenda." The lady said, "Glenda, you were right, my aunt died eight hours later." I said, "Excuse me, I wouldn't have said that. I may have said when she passes over or something on that order." She says, "What I mean is, I went to see my aunt in the hospital. I told everyone about your reading and describing who was standing around my aunt. She passed eight hours later and we were all relieved that we knew who was there to help her cross over." I said, "Well there is a big difference in that story then me saying your aunt was going to die."

A few months ago I was giving a professional reading. I had the lady's grandfather in spirit. I asked, "Who is Danny?" She said, "That is my uncle here." I said, "I see him going into a bar room and grandpa follows him in there." I feel like grandpa is with him for love and support a lot of times." She said, "That makes sense Uncle Danny drinks a lot. I am glad to know my grandpa is with him." The following week my assistant called. She asked, "Do you remember the lady you gave the reading to last week? Danny passed away. The family was relieved to know grandpa in spirit would be with him to help him cross over." Again, they were happy to know a relative in spirit was with their loved one when they crossed. I honestly did not see that this person was going to pass. I just saw it as grandpa was with this particular family member as in love and support.

The Reverend had taught a class on the code of ethics. I have had the readings where I would sense death coming and feel my face turn white. It felt like I was losing the color in my face. This happened about a month ago. I was talking to a friend about her family member that was in the hospital. I felt and sensed that the relative would not be returning home. I felt my face go white. This is someone who knows me very well and is very intuitive herself. She just has not tuned it in. I saw the tears well up in her eyes. I hadn't turned away from her fast enough. I guess she knew by the look on my face. I said, "Just know your loved ones will be there, even if it is ten years from now." I named the loved ones in spirit who would be there for her. I told her, "Call me if you need me at anytime day or night." Her loved one did not come home from the hospital alive.

In a very large group reading, I was asked about a relative that was terminally ill. She wanted to know how long her relative had left to live. I was surprised by the question. I said, "I wouldn't give you that information if I knew it." She said, "You wouldn't?" I caught myself and what I was saying. I said, "What I mean is that I don't believe spirit would give me that type of information." I said, "My suggestion to you would be, spend as much time with your loved one as possible. Don't treat them any different then you ordinarily would. When you feel their pain and suffering is unbearable and they want to go home (to Heaven) then help them cross. You do this by telling them it is okay to go. I know this is not an easy thing to do. Many times we have our own selfish reasons for wanting to keep them here with us. We never want to lose them but out of love and support for our loved one, it is best to let them go."

ALA, My Niece

ALA has been very much a part of my journey. At one time, my own family was so hard on me about my being a psychic medium that I was going to give it up. ALA, my niece, was one of the few people that believed me and she believed in me. When my journey into the psychic medium awareness started, I practiced with ALA's grandmother and mother. ALA was very tuned into this. I had gotten permission from ALA's father and mother to give her a book for teenagers about the psychic medium awareness. It was for her sixteenth birthday. The famous medium had written it.

ALA called me one day to ask a question about the psychic medium awareness. I said, "ALA, I am giving it all up. I am not fighting with everyone anymore over this." ALA started crying. I started crying. ALA said, "No Aunt Glenda, I believe in you." We talked quite awhile about this. Needless to say, I never gave up studying.

ALA was the one who assisted me with the first practice group reading I had done. I read for about eight people there. The lady I was supposed to do my very first practice reading for was there this time. My focus was for her mostly. I knew this before the reading. While I went in to meditate, ALA assisted me by getting them comfortable and relaxed. She got them bottled water and then led them through a breathing exercise known as the prana exercise.

I had gone to the back bedroom in my mother's house to meditate. It was then that I realized I hadn't brought the materials I normally used to open to spirit communication with me. I was nervous. I wondered, would I be able to do this without the famous medium's tape that I always used? Two other things I didn't bring with me was the Energy Ball picture or the Jesus picture that Bjean had sent to me. I always used these things to meditate and connect with spirit. Unbelievably both had fallen over on the computer desk as I was grabbing for something else. I said, "No, I better not take them, I may forget to bring them back home." ALA had called me and was rushing me. I had a Chat Event to be at that morning doing Absent Healing Prayer. I wasn't thinking straight. I just had to do everything by memory. As I got to the third chakra, I could see the Energy Ball and the Jesus picture that Bjean had sent me sitting on my computer desk. I was also worried about Precious Pup (my little doggie), she wasn't feeling well. I saw her laying down sleeping. I continued to open my chakras all the way. Then, I went in and started reading. It all went very well.

Later, ALA and I had a quarrel and we weren't speaking. I hadn't heard from her in over two weeks. My mom was in Florida. It was on Mother's Day. I had professional readings to do. I was on that spiritual high when I got home from the readings. I needed to call my mom in Florida to wish her a Happy Mother's Day. I called and after my mother and

I had been talking for awhile, she said, "I was in tears this morning." She said, "ALA had been in an accident and got burned." She had called ALA's father and thought he said she would be fine. My mom thought what got burned was both her legs.

I hung up the phone. The next thing I know I look to my left with my third eye. That is the way you would go over the bridge to Virginia where ALA was. I saw the hospital bed with ALA in it. I could see her face wrapped up in white bandages. I saw her fiancé sitting in a chair by the bed with his face in his hands. He had his arms propped on his legs. I am shaking my head thinking, "It sure looks like to me there is more wrong than just her legs." I talked to ALA a day or two later on the phone and I described to her what I had seen. She validated it as being correct. I described exactly where her fiancé was sitting and also what direction the bed was positioned. I also told her who in spirit was there with her. Later that day when I talked to ALA's mother, I told her what spirit loved ones were with her for love and support. ALA and I made amends. It was then that I learned, whatever the disagreement, it is not worth arguing to that degree. During this time, I had called my brother, ALA's dad. I could read his mind. I could hear the tears in his voice. He started to say something but didn't. What he wanted to say was, "If you are so (Bleep) Psychic then why didn't you know this was going to happen?"

I had actually picked up a little on the accident, prior to the accident, so had ALA, and ALA's mother had had a dream vision. ALA stopped to see me. She wanted to show me her new Angel Cards and to do an Angel Card Reading for me. ALA was sitting in a chair right next to me in the computer room. She was talking about where they were going that week-end. I started thinking that is dangerous. I told ALA this and went on and to say some very strange things. I said, "Well do you have to go there? Can't you stay at home while they go to the shooting range?" I felt fear with this. ALA looked at me like I was acting weird. ALA said, "Come on Aunt Glenda let me give you an Angel Card Reading." I said, "OK." That broke the connection I was picking up on. ALA gave me the reading.

When ALA got home from the hospital I went over to her house to give her hands on Reiki. After the Reiki session ALA brought out a stack of pictures that had been taken at the hospital. They were exactly like what I had been seeing.

Spirit works with us in so many ways. Spirit was trying to get the message through. I thank God and all of his Angels, for today ALA is doing well. I am thankful for all the Absent Healing, Reiki, and Prayers sent for her and all the others injured in the fire.

ALA has also read Michael Tamura's "You Are The Answer." ALA, I always felt was more to the Healing part of the Awareness. I feel she would do awesome in Reiki healing.

ALA and her grandma nick named Granny came to visit me one day. We were standing looking at my china hutch. I looked at ALA and she had this warm golden glow around her. She put off this awesome heat. I rarely ever saw anyone's Aura but I saw ALA's. I looked at ALA again for this didn't go away. I asked her, "ALA are you pregnant?" She gave me a dirty look and said, "I don't hardly think so." She looked back at the china hutch and then back at me and asked, "Am I?" I said, "We will see, won't we?"

Some time had gone by when I was talking to one of my

family members and they said, "ALA is pregnant." I didn't think anything about it until I hung up the phone. I sat and tried to figure out exactly how long it had been since Granny and Ala was over visiting me.

I called ALA and I asked her how long ago it had been since she was here with Granny. She said, "It has been about three months." I asked, "Ala how many months pregnant are you?" She said, "Three months." We both laughed and she wanted to get off the phone and go tell Granny.

ALA had a very hard pregnancy and delivery. Everyone around the Spiritual chat rooms sent healing, Reiki, and prayers out to her and the baby. Michael and Raphaelle Tamura were there behind the scenes. They kept ALA and Baby in their healing basket of prayers. They put my name in the healing basket also. I needed strength to hold it together.

I had picked up on ALA would be having trouble but I really thought it was my own fear. I thought I had fear for ALA because her cousin had similar difficulties giving birth to her son. This is exactly what I was picking up, that ALA was going to have similar complications.

When I found out ALA was having these difficulties, I just sat down and started crying. It wasn't until then that I told ALA about my visions. ALA said, "Aunt Glenda, always trust what you get."

I had done a reading for ALA's mother when she let me practice on her. One day she asked me, "Will I ever be a grandmother?" I said, "Yes, you will. I see a grandson for you. ALA will be of age. I say around eighteen or nineteen years old." I also told ALA that she was going to have a son. I hadn't remembered the reading to her mother until after I told ALA that she was going to have a boy.

My Long Time Friend

The meditations in the Meditation Room, I continued to look forward to. Before I knew anything about the psychic medium awareness, one of my long time friends passed.

She had Hepatitis C. I was furious when I heard that her husband had the doctors pull the plug. Originally, she had a living will written up saying she didn't want to live on machines alone. At the end, she couldn't breathe on her own and she had a feeding tube. I always wanted to go see her at the hospital but never got the opportunity.

She was in New Jersey and I never had the money and always had to work. She could write to you by holding a pencil in her mouth and using it to type what she wanted to say on a computer. Knowing this made me realize she was very much aware of what was going on. She was in a nursing home type environment and there were many other things going on with her medically. My longtime friend started crying when her husband told her that the following day they would be pulling the plug. She typed on the computer,

"I will die then won't I?" She had long before that told them she didn't want to die and didn't want them to pull the plug. She had changed her mind.

I thought it was strange when I was telling my brother Marty on the phone that she had passed. He said, "Well that is really weird. I had a dream about her the Saturday before." The Saturday before was when she passed. I had asked her to check on Marty now that she had gone to Heaven. She may have heard my thoughts.

I was still furious over this. That Christmas I even sent a Christmas card to her husband's address. I wanted him to remember her. I had already received a letter from him with her obituary, a picture, and her prayer card from the funeral. I knew she had passed but I sent the Christmas card anyway. He even called me several times. Again, I wasn't yet aware of the psychic medium awareness. He informed me that she indeed would always be with him. He had her cremated and took the urn with him everywhere he went. He went on to say, "I feel her around me and know she is with me."

I came home from work one day very anxious for the meditation class. Often I would be tired, my body hurting, and frustrated about life. The meditations always refreshed me. They took the soreness from work away from me, rejuvenated me, and left me feeling good.

I don't remember who led the meditation that day. They led us to a bakery shop. Today we were working with smells. I know one thing the bakery smell was so strong and for a minute I felt sick from the sweet smell. Today, as always, my brother Joe was there and my long time friend was sitting there. The one leading the meditation had us sitting in the bakery at one of the tables.

My long time friend was beautiful and young again. She

had her long hair back. It was almost to her waist like it was when I first met her. In her picture that her husband had sent me she had cut all her hair short. She had donated her long hair to children who have cancer to make them a wig. The two of them sat with me in the bakery shop.

I had also seen her with Joe in a dream vision. I knew they were bringing me the message that she was doing fine. Many of these stories come back later in my journey. My friend has come through in practice readings also. This is more validation that spirit lives on.

ASTRAL TRAVEL

I had heard others talk and ask questions about Astral Travel at the spiritual chats. I had also read about it on the Message Board at one of the sites I went to. I didn't know much at all on the psychic medium study and I knew even less about Astral Travel. I have studied it somewhat but find it to be complicated. I don't really know why or how I get there when I Astral Travel.

Every time I would think of something I said, "No, I don't want to go there," and I would go there when I fell asleep. I just read and heard that we travel in the Astral World when we sleep. I would wake up totally embarrassed when I woke up and realized I had visited places where I had no business being.

That was what the answer to my question that day when I went to see the famous medium in Virginia. That was how I got to Martha's Vineyards the night of the famous young man's fatal plane crash. I had finally found out the answer to what was a nightmare to me for so many years.

When this started happening a lot, I started apologizing

a lot. I said, "I don't know how or why this is happening." I went to the famous medium's website to the chat log section. There I looked for all the chat events about Astral Travel. I found several chat events on this subject. I came to know that is how we meet our loved ones in dream visits. This happened to me many times in my meeting loved ones.

When that would happen to me earlier, I thought I was dreaming about their passing. I later learned I was actually astral traveling and would see them when I was returning home.

I went to see Bjean in Astral Travel once. I wanted to ask her a question about the psychic medium awareness. I was way above her and she was walking very fast. I was feeling as though she was running late for a class that she was taking. I said, "Bjean, I have a question to ask you." Bjean didn't answer me. I was upset and my feelings were hurt. I later told Bjean about this.

Another time, I was watching a television show that aired about the famous medium I had been to see. He was doing a show on the Queen Mary. I fell asleep on my couch. The next thing I know I am sitting on a couch and the famous medium was sitting in a chair. I had this little girl sitting on my lap. I wondered why she was there and where she came from. I wondered why I was there. The thought came, "She is here to get a reading." It was weird because the little girl was sitting in my lap. I felt like she was too close to me. Again, I couldn't understand where she came from and why she was sitting in my lap. My next thought was, "Well maybe after she gets a reading, maybe he would give me a reading."

I heard this in thoughts when this was taking place from the famous medium to me and from me to him. I don't remember hearing words. I just heard thoughts. I felt as though I shouldn't be there. I got the feeling that it was an invasion of privacy. Then I felt loving thoughts and I thought this was probably the healing for the little girl.

A lady comes in the room from a doorway up at the far end of this room. She has a little girl with her. The little girl looked about nine years old. I felt the lady may be a friend or relative of his. They come over and sit on the couch with me. They hug me and I feel this overwhelming love come from them.

I went into the chat room and I told the famous medium's room operators what had happened. I told them, "I am so very sorry. I didn't mean to do that. I don't know how I got there. I also don't know who that little girl was or why I had taken her there to get a reading." His Ops are very smart. They talked to me calmly about it. I was upset but they weren't. They asked, "Who was the little girl." I said, "I don't know where she came from. She was just there." I told the Ops that I thought he was giving her a reading. I told them I thought maybe I could get one afterwards. "The Ops asked me if that could have been the little hurt girl inside me?" Again I told them, "I don't know who she was or how she got there. I just felt she was way too close to me."

Today, I am pretty sure this famous medium was not giving some little girl a reading in my Astral Travels. I believe it was me, the little girl me, who was abused, who was hurt so many times as a child. I even posted this on his site message board about a year ago but he never acknowledged this. Whether real or not, this happened and I feel it was real. That bothered me a very long time.

I had also Astral Traveled to see Raphaelle and Michael not long ago. I emailed Raphaelle and described the surroundings that I saw. I also told her what I had heard. I later apologized. I said, "I am so sorry if I was there." Raphaelle said, "No problem Glenda; we are use to having Spirit in the house." What was so odd about this was I had heard a spirit talking to me. This I laugh about now but it wasn't funny then. When I realized I had talked to a spirit while in Astral Travel, I was scared. I thought to myself, "Why am I scared about that? I was talking to spirit all the time." About this time I started realizing some of these thoughts were spirit asking me questions and at other times answering my questions. I feel this happened here.

Another time, I went to see my friend Maja in Astral Travel. I saw Maja in her car. She has a young woman with her that looked much like her. I thought this was her sister. They were rushing to go somewhere. Not long after that, I gave Maja, Duki her mom, and cousin a private reading in Heaven On Our Side's chat room, AngelsLanding. Maja validated everything I told her that I saw, heard, and felt. I told her that I felt they were in a hurry. She told me exactly where they were rushing to. Her sister lived somewhere else and was visiting her hometown. They were rushing to get to a memorial mass for their father.

The Reverend suggested that I ask my guides to take me to places of learning. He said, "Ask your Guides to take you to the Akashic Records. That way you won't be in all these places you aren't supposed to be."

I had visited a mutual friend of ours who was ill. He told me sometimes we go to check on friends after sending them Absent Healing. I often asked for distant healing for her. I practiced what he suggested.

Before I fell asleep, I would ask my Angels and Guides to surround me and to only let me go for higher learning. I said, "Maybe places like the Akashic Records." It happened; I was at the Akashic Hall of Records. I had this book in my hand. I put the book back. I was in spirit form. I opened what looked like a locker to me. I put this overcoat like wrap around me. My thought was, "This is my body and I have to put it back on before I go back home." When I woke up, I didn't remember what the book said." Whenever I talked to my guides for learning, I couldn't remember what was said. I always felt my soul knew though.

I remember very vividly another time of being at the Akashic Hall of Records. I was on my way back. It was like I was flying downward. I was in a straight up and down position and flying straight up and down. I was coming downward. I was asking a question concerning what I had seen in the book that I was reading. I was given an answer. When I received the answer, I was smiling even though it wasn't the answer that I wanted to hear. The details I will not share for it is too personal and was for my information only.

*I find out later the wife and sister in the fatal plane crash were passed. They just hadn't crossed over yet. I was in my spirit body and that is how they saw me there. You will have to google online or read more on this subject of fast passing. This topic is another whole book.

THE DREAM PREMONITIONS

As time went on and I learned more about the psychic medium awareness, I would remember a lot of strange things that happened in the past. These experiences were no longer strange to me.

I remember dream premonitions from the time I was about eighteen years old. The first one I remember having was where my father was flying through the air. I could see the vehicle but the driver's face was blurred so I couldn't tell who was driving. I still didn't understand the dream. I woke up shaking all over and sweat pouring off me. I sat on the side of the bed and tried to understand what I had dreamed about.

I do know my biological father was in the hospital with pleurisy. My long time friend said she would take me over to see him. For some reason, I had to go see him and make sure he was there.

Several years later, I found out what I had dreamed about. My father was in Eastern Shore Maryland working. He was a waterman at this time. My father was walking down the road when a car hit him. My seeing him flying through the air was from the impact of the car hitting him. The strangest part of this dream was that I was in the dream. I took off running when I saw the car hit him. I thought the car was going to hit me also.

I next had a dream that I see one of my brothers in a two car collision. I couldn't see his face for it was blocked out again. It looked blurred like they do on the news when they don't want you to see the person who is talking. I knew that it was one of my two living brothers that had a name that started with the letter J. I just didn't know if it was James or Joe.

I had another dream about this. This time in the dream I was seeing three caskets. The caskets were in a scene like Heaven. There were two next to each other. I was standing there looking at them and I knew this was my biological father and my brother Jimmy in spirit. The other was on the other side of this scene but I couldn't see who was in the casket. I knew it was not reference to my baby sister who was a miscarriage. I knew it was for someone who was going to die. In my dream, they did not ever let me see who was in the casket.

It ended up being my brother Joe who was killed in a two car collision. I had told my mom about the dreams earlier. What the dreams did not ever show me was when this was going to happen. When Joe was killed in the car wreck, my mom told me never to tell her about my dreams again.

The only other dream I had like this was my step dad's brother. I was in a funeral parlor. I walked up to the casket to see who was in it. As I was walking up to the casket, I thought it was my step dad. When I got up to it I realized that it was my step dad's brother. They looked so much alike. I told mom about my dream. She got mad at me. She said, "I thought I told you never to tell me about your dreams again." I felt bad that I upset her. I honestly didn't believe the dreams. It was something I just didn't understand. It was about eight months later when my step dad's brother passed.

Before I knew about the psychic medium awareness, I was searching for someone. My mother had been married before. She lied about her age so her adopted parents had the marriage annulled. My mother later gave birth to a baby girl when she was 14 years old. Without my mom's knowledge, her adopted parents had the baby adopted out. Legally, they could do so because my mom was still a minor child at the time.

I used to cry wondering if I would ever find her. I had a copy of the book that told you what Big Hugs did to find adopted children. I searched on the internet. I searched public records. I spent hours looking through files. I even had a friend of mine look for records where she lived because she lived where my half-sister was born. The records were sealed. It wasn't until after the following year of her birth that they no longer sealed adoption records.

My mother was adopted or so we thought but that is another story to be told in another book. Her biological family had searched for her over the years until finally they were reunited after fifty-years with the help of the Big Hugs Organization. I do believe my biological uncle's daughter in Heaven made this happen.

We never met my mom's biological mother. She had passed before the family was reunited. However, I was crying one night looking at a picture of my biological grandmother. I asked my grandmother, "Will I ever find her – my sister?"

One night soon after, I had a dream. I saw two of my grandmother's in spirit and in the middle was the long lost sister. I never realized what that meant, until I later found her. I knew my grandmothers were helping me, yet I still did not understand the meaning of this.

I still have dreams that I don't understand at the time I am having them. They only come to light after they happen.

I once had a dream. In that dream there was a storm. I was trying to call my mom. She wasn't answering her phone. My psychic eye took me to a house across the bridge where one of my brothers lived. I said, "She must be over visiting my brother" but I knew that the house I was seeing in my dream wasn't the house where my brother lives. I couldn't understand why my mom was at this house across the bridge. I also couldn't understand why my step dad wasn't with her. My psychic eye took me to my step dad's house. I didn't see him there either. I told my co-worker and friend Darlene about it. This dream comes to light later on in this book also.

I have had many dream premonitions like this in my life. The first time was in a dream I had and in the dream I saw on a dumpster with large numbers 197. They have lottery numbers where I live so I started playing that number and sure enough, I won. Sometimes I would dream a number and it would come out the opposite of the way I had seen it in my dream. I call that, number being mirrored. I don't count on this but I do play numbers if I have the money since I feel spirit gave me the number for a reason. My dream doesn't tell me when the number is going to come out, so a lot of times I would play it when I had money and then when I didn't have money to play the number, it would come out.

It was funny because in one of the recent group readings I did, a lady asked me if a certain number was ever going to come out. I said, "I couldn't ask that." She then said, "I did dream a number last night." Everyone in the room started laughing. I said, "There you go. They gave you a number to play." I told her how I had hit different numbers from seeing them in a dream. I also told her the only problem was I didn't know when it was coming out because they don't tell me that. You have to play to win I guess.

THE READINGS

The next stories will be about readings that I have done. There won't be names mentioned, just details and my experiences.

I am forever amazed at spirit and the communications. How they give me the information, truly is so unbelievable at times. Sometimes when I am given information in a dream vision I won't quite understand the message. On different nights, they will bring the dream vision in a different scenario until I get it right. If I need to take a nap, I often ask spirit to give me information on an upcoming reading in my dreams and they do.

When I am giving a reading and I do not understand what I am seeing, spirit will show me in different ways. The hardest part for me is discerning what I am seeing. I often tell everyone I am reading for that when visions are given to me during readings, it is like playing charades. The actual game of charades itself, I may have played one time in my life. Often I have thought, "I wish I had played charades more. If I had of played charades more, perhaps I could understand spirits better."

I love the connection with spirit and the healing it brings to others. When I do psychic medium readings, I know how they feel. They feel the same way I did when the world-renowned medium had brought my spirit loved ones to me at his seminar.

I have been reprimanded many times from my online teachers for the way I do readings. I will only do my readings in my own chat rooms so that I may do it the way that best works for me which is by describing to the sitter or (client as I prefer to say) what I am seeing, feeling, and hearing from spirit. This gives the client a general idea about the process of psychic medium awareness which is helpful to my clients as most of them have never had a reading done before. A lot of the teachers who have online practice readings do not allow this way of reading. They also want the sitter to say yes or no and validate the readings afterwards. Often if the room is full in order to move on to as many readings as the readers can do, you really don't have time for validation. I find a much closer and clearer connection not only with spirit but with the sitter "client" as well by doing it my way.

There is a lot that has happened during the readings and the information the way I was seeing it has confused me. I will explain what I mean here during some of the readings. In some of the online classes we were told not to say during a reading is there a J name around you. Saying this, I have often found when the one you are reading for says yes eventually spirit will get the names to you. Here with the names I have often been spot on and at other times I do not get any names. I have learned to not do this if I am unsure. To me a person getting the reading may be looking for a particular name and if you get the wrong name then that does not reflect well on the medium and could be discrediting. Here they have all the details except the name right. I tell the ones I read for that I am not good at names and if the name comes through spot on that is even better. Spot on means correct with the name or reading.

I will tell you my experience again when the world-renowned medium put us in meditation. I saw on a higher level my biological father, my brother Joe, my brother Jimmy, and my baby sister (who was a miscarriage my mother had thirty years prior to this vision). I was seeing my baby sister as a five year old. Why? I don't know why but I knew that was my baby sister that was a miscarriage. That is one part of this journey that I never doubted.

I even told my mother the story exactly the way I tell it here. I said she was peeking around Daddy's legs being bashful like. My mother says one of my other sisters did the same thing when she was around the same age. This same scene has come up in my readings.

First I am telling some that didn't know, miscarriages are spirit and they return to Heaven. Now, I am seeing a child a certain age and the miscarriage was long before that age. The only thing I can do is tell them the truth; I don't have the answer why and tell them what I had experienced.

I have given readings where I was correct on the age also. One reading I gave went like this. I was giving readings for two ladies. I said, "I see a young man twenty years old." The lady said, "I had an abortion twenty years ago this month." I described the young man's hair, height, and size." I asked,

"Does this resonate with the parents?" She said, "Yes, the father."

I then look at the other lady. I said, "I see a three-year-old boy in spirit with blonde hair and blue eyes." The lady burst out in tears. She said, "I had a miscarriage three years ago today." I said, "I know this is emotional." I felt the emotions myself. I asked my guides to remove the emotions from me so I could continue to read. I said, "Crying is healing and you are in need of this. Please continue to cry and let this out so you may start the process of healing."

I felt this lady had buried this deep within and it continued to hurt her and haunt her so to speak. She later emailed me and thanked me for bringing this out and helping her to be aware. She was already very much into the belief of psychic medium awareness and has since become a Reiki Master. She also works with animals and gives them Reiki.

We were in one of the largest group readings that I had given yet. No one said anything from the ones I was sitting by reading at this time. Everyone kept saying "No" when I said, "Accident and alcohol related." This lady was sitting on the other side of the room; she said, "I can take the accident and alcohol related passing." She comes and sits in the chair in front of me. I put my focus only on her and block out everyone else. I said, "I am seeing a beautiful seventeen-year-old young woman. She says she will soon to be eighteen years old." The lady said, "No." I kept hearing accident and alcohol, accident and alcohol, and the lady kept saying, "Yes." I said, "This is your daughter." She said, "Yes." I was totally baffled now. I knew what I was seeing; I also felt and knew by now that I was with this lady here in front of me. I turned my head to the right like waiting for the beautiful spirit young lady to help me here. I look at the lady I said how much younger. She said her daughter had been hit by a car when she was six years old. I look back toward the spirit young lady and she starts to show me a memorial which I described, and her mother said, "Yes. We put a memorial up where she was hit by the car." The spirit young lady shows me herself at the age of twelve years old. Her daughter then tells me and shows me what her mother was doing here if the daughter was that age. The mother validates all of this with "Yes." Next, I am shown what the mother was doing when the daughter would have been fifteen years old. Her Mother said "Yes". This mother was crying the whole time. I really had to keep myself centered for this reading, I felt like falling apart crying myself. I stayed focused and centered.

Her daughter shows me once again her at the age seventeen soon to be eighteen years old. I just close my eyes and look at her daughter. Finally, I look at the mother. I said, "How long ago was this that the car hit your daughter." She said, "Eleven years ago." My mouth dropped. I know my expression had to be a sight. I was in disbelief of what was just brought through. I look at the daughter in spirit then back to her mother. I said," The daughter would be seventeen years old then, correct?" She said, "Yes" and her tears came even harder as she shook her head up and down the whole time. I then asked the mother "Is her birthday coming up soon? I have the feeling within the next two months." Her mother shakes her head up and down again and says, "Yes," and was crying even harder. I asked, "Would she have been eighteen years old?" The mother said, "Yes." I said, "There you are then."

I then close my eyes again and re-center myself. I had just about lost my balance. This was way too emotional for me. I once again describe the beautiful young woman in spirit. The mother said, "Yes. That is what she would have looked like." The daughter said, "Mom, I am all grown up now." The daughter wanted me to give her mother a hug. I got up and hugged her mother. As I did this I said, "Mommy, I have never left you." This was once again said in the little girl voice. Daughter had showed her mother in this reading, she was with her the whole time. She told her mother exactly what her mother was doing at the age of the certain years she would have been. She wanted to prove to her mother that she is with her. I hugged the mother and through the tears she smiled at me. I said, "You need much healing here. Please cry and release some of this." I told her that I wanted to try to help her more. I really wanted to give her a private reading and work with her one on one. This was her first reading of any kind. Everyone in the room was quiet. I never heard anything or anyone during the whole reading. I thought that since there were twenty or more people in the room we would have had some distraction.

Bjean had taught me how to block everything else out. I once was doing a meditation with Bjean leading the meditation when two men were working right underneath the house where my computer chair sits. They were making a lot of noise but I managed to do the meditation.

I also often wondered where I came up with some of the things I did. It sounded more like a counselor than the uneducated me. I knew it had to be the Divine Guidance from above. I just know I didn't have that type of intellect in the human form.

The Sisters

O ne reading I gave was for sisters. One sister had bought the other sister a reading from me as a Christmas gift. I knew nothing except they were sisters. The sister who purchased the reading introduced herself. The other sister had no idea what the gift was that she was getting as it was a surprise until she got there. I looked at the other sister and said; "I am your Christmas gift. I am going to give you a reading." She was very happy about this and hugged her sister and me at the same time.

As always, I was nervous. The words I had been told by Raphaelle Tamura, "If you don't believe in yourself, believe in spirit" ran through my mind over and over. Those words of encouragement helped me often in the days to come.

I always start by telling them about how my journey started with the seminar. How I studied materials to tune in my gifts. How there were no development circles or spiritual churches here. I always ask them if they ever watched any of the professional mediums on television. When they say "Yes", I am very fortunate for they have a general idea about psychic medium reading. It was also good to find out if the clients have had a reading before. These two young ladies were familiar with what to expect.

I felt right away that the one sister who needed more healing awareness was the sister who bought the reading for the other sister. I will share some of this reading. I had brought the mother through; one sister had asked me if she could ask a question. I said. "Sure you can. We can see if spirit will answer." She looked at me and asked, "Can you ask our mother in spirit if we will find out the information that we are looking for?" I closed my eyes and looked closer at the mother in spirit. Right away the mother shows in a vision of a computer and I am hearing research. I look at the sister and tell her what I am seeing. I told her, "Your mother said that you would be able to find out the information doing research on the computer." Then I say to her, "I am hearing the word adoption." Both sisters looked at each other surprised. The sisters were in disbelief that I had actually brought that through. I also told them that I didn't need to ask your mother the question. She heard you. She can hear your thoughts as well. That is how you bring your spirit loved ones to you. Finally, the sister who had bought the reading said, "Yes, I am adopted." The question they were wondering about was would they be able to find other relatives.

Then, I see a male father figure and I bring all this through. I asked "Is this both of yours father?" One sister said, "I don't know. Will he tell you if he is my father also?" the father spirit said, "Anyone can father a child not everyone can be a dad." I looked at both sisters and asked "Does this make sense to you." They said, "Yes very much so." The sister who was adopted knew they both had the same mother.

What they wanted to know was if they both shared the same father. The father who raised her as his child made it very clear from the other side that he was her dad.

I then turned to the sister the reading was bought for and her mouth started dropping. I had brought through her mother-in-law whom she was very close with. They both were very pleased with their readings. In the reading, the mother-in-law described much of the one sister's husband. We had taken a break and stepped outside. I then start giving them both psychic details during the break.

The sisters updated me on this reading many months later. They had found some of their family members in other states. They found most of the information on the computer.

During the readings, I kept seeing a white furry cat. Neither one of the sisters could understand what that meant at the time. I said, "Hold that thought or jot it down. Perhaps later on you may find out why I kept seeing this white furry cat." The one sister contacted me later to tell me about her visit with one of the new found relatives. As she sat on the couch talking to her relative, she saw a porcelain white furry cat sitting right in front of the couch.

ANGEL CARD READINGS

Another reader who had her own chat room gave me my very first Angel Card Reading. I wasn't doing readings myself at the time because I had taken a break. I was in one of my many downward spirals. What it really was is that my life had become unbalanced and I had let fear come back into my life. At the time of the reading, I thought anything at all would be comforting. I didn't believe Angel Card Readers could really see Angels. How I could ever think this was not possible sure beats me. Here I was talking to dead people. Jesus is my Master Guide and I am thinking Angel Card Readings aren't real which seems hypocritical of me.

She drew the cards for me. One of the cards she called Arch Angel Michael. I had heard about Arch Angel Michael but I did not really know anything about him. I didn't know what he looked like either. She read to me what the card said. She goes on to tell me how special Arch Angel Michael is and how he was there to protect me from the negative and from your own fears. She spoke how special it was to have an Arch Angel Michael's card drawn for you. I thought to myself, "She is right about both of these things. I need protection from negative thoughts. I also had a lot of fears."

The next time I did my meditation to connect with spirit. I said, "Okay Arch Angel Michael, if you are here please show yourself to me." I see this man dressed funny. He has a sword and a shield. I could understand Arch Angel Michael having a shield to protect me, however I thought to myself, "No way this is right. An Angel doesn't need to carry a sword." I figured I still had negative energies around me. I proceeded to reverse the meditation and close down my charkas properly.

Months later I went to another chat room where the reader was giving a lady a reading. In this reading she says, "Arch Angel Michael is around your son. He is there to protect your son." The reader goes on to describe what Arch Angel Michael looks like. I am staring at the computer screen and my mouth dropped wide open. This reader described Arch Angel Michael with a sword to cut away all that is negative. I could not believe what I was reading. I truly did see Arch Angel Michael. I went on to tell them my story and experience with the meditation and asking Arch Angel Michael to please show himself.

After the chat event, I went and typed into my browser Arch Angel Michael. I just stared. There was that funny outfit, sword, and the shield. This was too amazing. Once again, I think of how narrow-minded I truly was being. I can see Jesus for he is my Master Guide but I couldn't believe I actually saw Arch Angel Michael.

Later on in my journey, I had bought a deck of Angel Cards and decided I would try this so we had Practice Angel

Card Readings at my chat room. The first time I did Angel Card Readings, I felt that I was just reading the cards. The second or third time we had Practice Reading Class, I saw the Angels when I was reading for someone. I couldn't believe this but it was happening. What really amazed me was one time when I drew four cards. I explained to the ones I am reading for what their Angels looked like. I would then draw the Angel Cards. I started noticing that if I saw two women and one man Angel, the cards that were drawn was two women and a man Angel.

A lot of the readers would have the clients to give them the numbers of which card they wanted. I rarely ever did this. The only time I did this is if I sensed this is what I should do. I let the Angels show me or tell me which cards to draw. One of the Angels would often point to a card if I was unsure which card they meant.

I would have Practice Reading Classes with One Card of Guidance Angel Card Readings. The reason being, I didn't get to read for a lot of the chat family drawing three cards. After doing this a few times, I noticed spirit would come in so I started using this technique. I would draw the card of guidance to center enough to do the reading to bring spirit loved ones through. I was amazed at this.

Spirit Mom,
Got The Message Through

I hadn't been to work in about two weeks. When I had left work, Darlene's mother was in the hospital. I knew what this spirit lady looked like. She was one of my very first practice readings I had given from a picture. I knew pretty much about the family by now. Darlene was one of the few people that let me practice read for her.

At this time I had Practice Reading Class on Thursdays. Practice Reading Class is when a lot of mediums would get together and take turns doing readings for the chat family. It was Thursday, February 5th and one of the readers there said, "I have a lady in spirit." She goes on to describe her, name, description, personality, and descriptions of family still here. The name was not a common name. I didn't say anything at first. The spirit lady's name was Opal. One of the chat families had asked if this could be reference to the stone Opal and the month for that stone. The reader said, "No, I do believe this is a name." I said, "I do believe this reading is for me. I don't know if she has passed or not. She was in ICU when I was last at work. The reader then asked if I knew what she looked like. I said, "Yes, She is the very first lady I ever did a picture reading for and her daughter is my friend and co-worker. The reader went on and brought through more details and a message. I thanked the reader and explained to her how this would be an unusual way to find out my friend's mother passed.

It was Wednesday, almost a week later. I had been writing some sketch stories for this book and was taking a short break. I had the radio on and heard an obituary announcement for the passing of Opal and said her last name. Now I only knew Darlene's mother by her first name and she is the only person I knew of with the name Opal. The radio announcement named the Funeral Home that this Opal would be at and said that she had passed last Thursday so I went to the website to see if it listed my co-worker Darlene as Opal's daughter and it did. I then checked the calendar to see what the date was for last Thursday. I could not believe what I was seeing. Opal had passed February 5th. I had no prior knowledge of her passing. There was no way the reader could have known any of this information. The reader lived in another state. This state was a long way from where I live. The reader had no knowledge of my co-worker Darlene.

I immediately contacted the chat room owner and asked her to please go back and email me a copy of the chat log. I validated the reading with all the information that I had learned that day. I made copies of the reading. The chat logs were time stamped with the date on it. This was even more validation that this reading was authentic.

I went back to work. It was less than a week since Opal's passing. Darlene was at work. I said, "Darlene I have something very unbelievable and special for you. I have made extra copies for other family members of yours just in case they want a copy. You may not want to open this until you get home." I didn't want to upset Darlene at work. Darlene agreed with me that she wanted to wait until she got home. I had given a very short version of what had happened. I said, "Darlene, that was a very unusual way to find out your mother had passed. I am so sorry for your loss. Your mother has gotten her message through to you. You will see it in the chat logs."

Do you see how cleaver Mom was here in all this? Had she come to me personally, Darlene might have thought I was just trying to make her feel better. Mom Spirit brought the message through to Darlene in a way she knew could not be misunderstood in any way.

ONE IN A MILLION FRIEND

I called him my one in a million friend. I had seen him maybe once or twice in a bar. Years later, I met him in Alcoholics Anonymous. It had been so long ago that he didn't remember meeting me before.

I had went back out and started drinking again several times before getting sober this last time and staying sober. We call it a relapse. I later dated this friend for a while. He helped me stay sober many times along with other friends in Alcoholics Anonymous.

We stopped dating. Even though we weren't dating anymore, we stayed friends and kept in constant contact. He would call just to see how I was doing. I would see him often at my work when he would come into shop. He always took time out to say hello and update me on what was happening in his world. I still called him my one in a million friend.

He had twenty years of sobriety in Alcoholics Anonymous. He gave a helping hand to many around him. I am one of those he helped many times. My one in a million friend had a good sense of humor. He always had an easy going style about him.

One evening my mom called me to see if I could get a pack of cigarettes to her. Mom had quit smoking. She did not want my step dad to know she had started back smoking. I called my one in a million friend. I explained to him what was happening and asked him if he could please get a pack of cigarettes to my mom. I said make sure you don't let Pa see you give them to her. He laughed and said, "I just left there. We have been playing cards. It will look funny me coming back so soon but I will think of something." I got ready and went on to work.

The next morning I called my mom and asked her if she had a visitor. She said, "Yes, he came in and went into the bathroom. He left the cigarettes in there on the sink." He went into the kitchen and whispered to my mom where they were. On his way out the door, he had to walk past Pa. He told Pa, "When I was here earlier I forgot and left my girlfriend's picture here." Pa just looked at him strangely and smiled. My friend just walked on out the door.

My friend had battled cancer for quite awhile. He called me and said, "I go up to the hospital Friday. They are going to tell me if they can do anymore for me or not." He had called to make sure I was okay. He wanted to know how my car was running. He wanted to know if I needed anything. I told him I was fine and so was the car. I told him he just needed to take care of himself. For a very long time I always ended our conversations with, "We love you." By that I meant not only me but also my family.

A week later, I received a phone call from a family member of his. They called to tell me that my friend was in the hospital and wasn't doing well. I said, "I will take a shower and be right there." I was getting clothes together to wear. As I reached into the closet to get some jeans and a blouse I hear, "You don't have time enough to take a shower." I said out loud, "Okay I am coming right now then." I threw on my clothes really fast and drove just a few minutes up the street to the hospital.

I wasn't there fifteen or twenty minutes and my one in a million friend passed away right before my eyes. In all my life, I had never had this happen. I was in a state of shock.

His family let me have a few minutes to say bye for now. I told him in thought form, "I know you can hear me. I am going to miss you but it is okay to go home now." I walked out of the door and as I was walking to my car I said, "Jesus, Please take care of him and please take care of his family." I knew there was nothing I could do to help them.

I got online and saw that the Reverend was online. I sent him an instant message that I really needed to talk to him. He answered me. I told him what happened. He talked to me for a few minutes. The Reverend brought him through right away. My friend had a name you rarely heard of. The Reverend picked up on even his name.

I was tired but Psychic Medium Chuck Bergman was doing a Special Chat Event at one of the Professional Chat Rooms. I didn't want to miss it. Chuck Bergman also brought him through.

The next morning Jessica and I met in AngelsLanding. Jessica said, "Glenda he is here." Jessica goes on to describe exactly where I was sitting in the hospital. Just before my friend passed, I sensed he was standing to the right of my chair. He was in a coma. I knew he wasn't at that time in his body. Jessica described exactly where I saw him standing. I hadn't said a word about it to her. Jessica said, "Glenda, He says you told Jesus to take care of him." I had forgotten about it. I said, "Oh My Gosh, I did." I then told her that I had said that going out the door of the hospital to come home. Jessica says, "Glenda, during the prayers or the funeral you are going to see him."

I went to the prayers. When I got home I remembered what Jessica had said. I said, "I didn't see him." I had to get up early the next morning so I went to bed early.

The next morning after I took a shower I had washed the shower out with scrubbing bubbles. I forgot to put away the scrubbing bubbles. After I had put my makeup on, I picked up the hairspray to spray my hair. Well, at least I thought I had the hairspray. I had picked up the wrong can of spray and now had scrubbing bubbles all in my hair. I took a towel and wiped off the scrubbing bubbles as best I could. There was no time for me to wash my hair again for I had to leave right then and there to get to the funeral.

Just as I got to the church where the mass was being held, it started to rain. I went on in and sat down next to my step sister's husband and my friend's cousin. While we were waiting for the mass to start, I told my step sister's husband what had happened with the scrubbing bubbles. I was trying to break the sadness. I wasn't holding up very well at all. He said, "Glenda, I do believe you will be all right as long as it doesn't rain." I told him that it had started to rain hard as I was walking into the church.

Mass had started and I had just thought the thoughts, "Mass is almost over. Jessica said I would see him. I haven't seen him." I closed my eyes to say the prayer being said and there he was. He was standing right in front of the casket. What was so very strange about what I was seeing was there was three of him. I didn't understand and to this day don't understand what I was seeing. One when he was a young man, the one of him in the middle was the one I knew the most, the heavyset man, and the last was him after cancer had taken its toll on him. He was a very thin and tired looking man. The man in the middle is who smiled that familiar smile and waved at me. Just then they started playing the hymn Amazing Grace and everyone got up to leave the church. I started crying then and couldn't stop. It was an uncontrollable cry. I just went out of the church and to my car. I left and didn't go to the graveside services or to the celebration of life reception afterwards.

Right after that the Reverend had his Practice Reading Class. The Reverend brought through a man talking about bubbles. He is saying a lot of tiny bubbles. I didn't say a word. I was too embarrassed. To this day I don't believe I ever told the Reverend about this incident with the bubbles. With the sense of humor my friend had, I just knew he got a good laugh out of this one. I wasn't going to let others know what I did. I felt strongly that was what the Reverend was picking up on.

*As I reread this I picked up on My One In A Million friend went back to the age that he was happiest at. The man in the middle who was sober and before cancer took over.

Susan Duval & Abstract Art

Abstract Art is how he brought his name through. I was seeing a picture hanging on the wall. I thought to myself that looks like Abstract Art to me. Maybe Susan likes abstract art. He showed me everything in the room. This was for details of the upcoming reading I was to give to Susan Duval. I was very nervous for I hadn't done too many phone readings at this time.

Chuck Bergman was doing a seminar in Philadelphia through Susan Duval Seminars. A short time later, Chuck sends me an email that said, "I have a friend you can do a practice reading for." I really wanted to practice and tune in my gifts more on doing phone readings. We set up a date and time for me to give Susan Duval a phone reading. I was amazed at her energies. She was a very beautiful and kind lady. Her energies were gentle. I immediately felt comfortable reading for her.

I said, "Susan I am seeing Art hanging on the wall. To me it looks like Abstract Art." I then ask, "Do you like Abstract Art?" Susan laughed and said, "Art is my true loves name." I thought that was an amazing way to bring Art's name through. I continued to bring through other details. I brought through Art's description and personality. I said, "Susan would there be any importance to the fact that I am seeing the Actor Robert Duval?" Susan said, "Art has a brother named Robert." I then proceeded to describe different rooms in her house. Next came birthdays and anniversaries. Spirit Art showed me scenes of places he and Susan had been. He also showed me different things they enjoyed. I didn't trust myself on this one. Art was talking to me about Edgar Cayce. I just went ahead and brought that through. Art told me right. Susan said they both loved learning about Edgar Cayce.

Abstract Art's Spirit has come back several other times over the years. When he did, I would email Susan and sure enough the details were correct. The most recent email reading I gave Susan is the one that really surprised me most.

At the time, I worked at night and slept during the day. It was my night off so I decided to update my website with the newsletters of well-known mediums and teachers. I was adding Susan Duval's newsletter and I kept hearing birthday and anniversary, birthday and anniversary. I thought I was hearing it from Abstract Art. So, I emailed Susan and said, "Please don't think I am crazy, but I was working on adding your newsletter to my website, when I started hearing over and over, birthday and anniversary. I was surprised when she emailed me back right away because it was wee hours in the morning. The email reading continued. She said, "Yes, I just had a birthday. Several days later will be the anniversary of my beloved Art's passing. I said, Susan he must have been standing right close to me because I was freezing. I almost went to get a coat out of the closet." Susan said, "I was chilly so I am sitting here at the computer with a coat on."

I told Susan, "What Art is talking about now I really do not want to bring through." Art had even brought through some of her health issues. Art had assured Susan that the health issues were minor. He wanted to assure her all would be okay. That, I do believe, was the first time I had brought through anything about medical issues. Even today I don't care to bring this type of information through. However, I was taught that I should bring through what spirit shows. Susan said, "Now I know why I was sound asleep, woke up and walked over to the computer because Art wanted to wish me a Happy Birthday."

All Spirit Loved Ones are very special I know. Abstract Art is very special. He seemed to know when I needed a little help. This reading here was right after my last downward spiral. My assistant had booked me for professional readings. I was worried about whether or not I would be able to do the readings. Art came and directed me to Susan. He new Susan was gentle and kind. He knew she would appreciate a reading also. Art did this several other times. He wanted me to see that I could do the readings in a few days. He was right, for I did the readings and everyone was happy with them

Art never came empty handed either. During the readings, he would always bring flowers for Susan. Different types of flowers and colors. Susan later told me that was because he always gave her flowers. He gave them so often that everyone used to call Art the Flower Man. Art's energies are always like that too when he comes through in the readings. He comes through as always being pleasant, strong, happy, funny and romantic. A romantic, is Abstract Art.

Art's Spirit continues to pop in now and then. One night I was playing poker for fun. Abstract Art shows up and says, "They are cheating." I laughed and thought I was just very tired. I emailed Susan and asked, "Susan did Art like to play poker?" I had told her in the email what had happened. I cut the computer off and went to bed. The next day when I went online Susan had emailed me back and said, "Yes, he used to play cards all the time." I thought, "Maybe I wasn't imagining that. Maybe they were cheating."

Group Readings

My Assistant, who wishes to remain anonymous, had booked me for a group reading. When she books the readings, she does not tell me anything except the day, time, location, and how many.

I had worked the night before and got off work at 7 A.M. EST. I was very tired and wondered that with so little sleep, would I be able to do a group reading? I just recalled the words of wisdom Raphaelle Tamura had said to me, "Glenda, if you do not have faith in yourself, believe in spirit." Once again her words were correct.

On the way to my Assistant's house, I hadn't turned the radio on in the car but kept hearing a song playing in my mind. It was a country music song and the words were, "I was a drinking man." I heard these words over and over again. Then, halfway there, my left leg began tingling, became numb, and started hurting. I wondered if it was from the night before at work. I soon realized the drinking man had a problem with his left leg. I would pick up on names that resonated with the readings, prior to the readings, as was the case this time.

Once I got there and everything was set up, I explained a little about the process and how the readings work. I then asked if anyone had ever had a reading. Several had been to a well-known medium's seminar but had not received a reading. Of course Mandy, my Mini Pet Assistant, met me at the car when I got there. I talked to her as we walked into the house together. I said to Mandy, "You know what time it is don't you?" She was all excited. She brought her fair share of Pet Spirit Loved Ones through during the readings.

I looked at everyone in the room. I started with one lady out of five. I described the gentleman that I was seeing. I go on and tell everyone about when I was driving to meet them for the readings. The song I had been hearing was for this gentleman. He had been a drinking man. I asked the lady I am reading for, "Did this gentleman have a problem with his left leg?" She said, "He had heart bypass surgery and they used a vein from his left leg." That was validated. I am very familiar with this type of surgery for my mother had heart bypass surgery. The reading goes on and spirit husband and father said, "Birthday." I said, "Your husband is telling me about a recent birthday or one coming up soon." She said, "My birthday is coming up soon. I hear, "Tell her in March." She said, "Yes." She asked, "Can you get him to tell you what date?" I started getting nervous. This was an unusual request. I felt the pressure. I closed my eyes to see spirit clearer. I asked, "Can you help me out here and tell me what date?" I told his wife that he said "It is on the fifteenth of March." She said, "Yes, that is correct." I then look at my assistant in disbelief. I couldn't believe that I was getting all of this accurate. I go on to describe many other things very accurately.

He shows me a dresser that has a big mirror over top of it. He said, "This dresser is in your room." He was still talking to his wife. His daughter was also here during the reading. He said, "One of the drawers had something of his in it." There was something that had belonged to him that was important to him. She will check when she goes home on this one.

I then move over to the other side of the room where there are two sisters. I bring their mother through. She was divorced from their father who was also a drinking man. He is still here. Mother in Spirit, once I made the stronger connection here, brought out the names I had been hearing on the way to the readings. The sisters validated the names to be correct. Mother in Spirit then brings through detail on their daughters. She described recent things her granddaughters had been doing. She described their personalities. Everything was accurate.

One of the ladies sitting next to the mother and daughter that I had read for was asking about her father who came through. While I was at home getting ready for the group reading, I had written down, "Peach." I heard, "Georgia Peach" also in thought form. I wrote that down. I later dismissed it shaking my head. I did not bring it through. It came out in this reading that this young lady was here from Georgia. She said her father used to carve crosses out of peach seeds.

Pet Spirit Loved Ones came through as well. There was a little doggie I kept seeing. I couldn't make a connection with this doggie right away. This little doggie was a white dog that looked something like Mandy my Assistant's little dog.

I said, "There is a little white dog here, a dog-named Mandy or someone named Mandy in spirit or here." There were no takers at the time. Finally, after many details and readings coming through, all were happy with their readings. I asked the group if they had any questions or if there was something else I could help them with for I was losing connection.

The lady I had first read for says, "I was hoping you would bring some more information through for my friend here." It was already established in the readings, that the friend with her was a long time friend of the family and like a sister to her. Father in Spirit brought this out in his message to his daughter and granddaughter that were here.

I had covered suicide quite a bit at the end. I was puzzled about this and started feeling that I was rambling. No one was speaking up about suicide or none had come through the readings so far. Finally, I ask again and my assistant says, "I was reading a story about a nineteen-year-old young man that committed suicide and sadly his father had committed suicide before then. I didn't feel I was with this part really, but it was very good to bring this out around the reading to follow.

I look at the friend of the family and I say who is it you wish to connect with; just give me a first name and the relationship. As soon as she said "my brother" I could see him. I had asked earlier, if anyone had with them something that belonged to their loved ones they wish to connect to. Everyone had said, "No." Now I say can you give me something that belongs to only you. She hands me a ring and said, "This was his, my brother in spirit." I just smiled. I then take the ring. I brought out confusion and accident. She said, "Yes to confusion but we don't know if it was suicide or an accident. Now I am confused, for she says I don't know.

She said, "Yes," when I said it was a drug overdose. She goes on to explain, "We don't know if he did it on purpose or if it was an accident." In all that followed, I kept getting that it was not done on purpose. I felt he took too many because he forgot he already took the medications. What was sad was this spirit brother had left behind a young son. I said to the friend and all the family members around this, "Do you have access to the young son and can you help him with this." Everyone there knew each other. They were close and vowed to help the young son still here in love and support.

I then go on and say, "In your journey, what you have learned here today from the readings, please help another in need." I then suggested some books that covered suicide. I also knew what I didn't understand earlier; why I covered suicide so much when no one was claiming it. It had come out in this reading. It also came out that the lady blamed herself and felt guilty thinking she could have prevented this. I went over this with her carefully. She had started crying as soon as I brought her brother through. I said, "You are the reason I am here. You have bottled all this up. You are keeping it inside because you are the pillar of strength for everyone else." Her best friend with her validated this to be true.

I have learned that when I do group readings, someone in the group needs much more learning and healing than the others. Don't get me wrong for we all need healing. There are just certain clients that need it more than the others.

I then said, "He is showing me a vision of you sitting on the side of the bed, toward the foot of the bed. He is hugging you and comforting you. The lady said, "The night he died, I had a dream that he came to see me. He, in my dream, was sitting at the foot of my bed." I said to her, "Please know that he did come to see you. This is what we call a Dream Visit."

Then I asked, "Is there a little dog, white dog, and is this dog's name Mandy?" She said, "Yes there is a little white dog. The dog's name was Candy." If spirit had of shown me candy I wouldn't have resonated it with a name but as candy itself. They brought it to me the best way they could. The name was close enough that I take that.

I was amazed at these readings. Here we had covered alcohol, drugs, and suicide. This is exactly what my book is about. Learning how to carry the message of experience, strength and hope to another. Not only the message in Alcoholics Anonymous but also in the Psychic Medium Awareness. As I always do, I cover the information about how you can learn and tune in the psychic medium awareness not only to do readings, but also to help you in your everyday lives.

Our Pet Loved Ones...

Now I Lay Me Down To Sleep …
Now My Soul Jesus Keeps …

Laddie Boy …

I had read about our pet loved ones crossing over in the first book I read of the famous mediums'. This was totally against what I had been taught all my life. Just the thought of this was awesome and made sense to me. I was told animals don't have souls and for this reason they could not go to Heaven. I could never figure out why they didn't. They have a heart, they lived, and they breathed like us humans.

Precious Pup and Laddie Boy were my ex-husband and my babies. We shared joint custody. When he would go away aboard ship, he would send me dog support while he was gone. When he was home he bought most of the food and we shared grooming and vet bills.

Shelley Duffy from the famous medium's resource page

gave me a reading. In this reading she said I see a white dog. She insisted it was a white dog and she said this dog will help you tune in your gifts. Precious Pup was blond in color. If we cut her fur short she looked more like a white dog.

I always called our Laddie Boy, my little psychic dog. He would come over to me at the computer while I was doing practice readings online. He would put his front paws up on my leg and stare me in the eyes. I would say, "What? Do you have a friend in the house?" What I meant was did you have pet spirit in the house? I would close my eyes to focus better and there would be pet spirit.

I didn't catch on to this until Laddie Boy had done this several times. Laddie Boy was a dark color he wasn't white. Precious Pup always barked when spirit was in the house and she wouldn't stop until I brought spirit through. Early on when doing meditation, I would see both our dogs in white light and ask their guides to come in, during spirit communication.

Laddie Boy had prostate cancer. When it was time to have him put to sleep, I couldn't do it. I told his vet, "You have to make the call I can't do it."

I had a very spiritual experience that day. I saw my family loved ones in spirit around me but I didn't see Jesus. I said, "Jesus you promised me that you would be here to take our Laddie Boy." Next thing I know I see Jesus step forward and take our Laddie Boy's Spirit body. I said, "But Jesus the vet hasn't given him the needle yet." The famous medium always said that we leave our bodies before death. The vet had taken tests on Laddie Boy. I had to make sure there was nothing more we could do for him.

Laddie Boy's vet, or so I thought it was the vet, said, "Glenda, we don't want this little dog to suffer." Now mind you, the vet had never called me by my first name. Second, I never saw the vet open his mouth while I was hearing that but it was a male voice. Jessica later told me it was my Brother Joe's voice I was hearing and not the vet as I had thought. I really didn't hear it in thought form. It was more in a voice I thought.

The vet came in with the needle. When the vet gave Laddie Boy the shot, I was holding him. I looked up and screamed, "Jesus help me." That poor doctor, I bet they could hear me all over the office. When Laddie Boy's body went limp, I felt a calm come over me. I waited for them to get Laddie Boy ready to take to where I needed to take him. I was in a state of shock and devastated but I coped. If I tried to tell you what this did to Laddie Boy's Daddy, I would have to write another book.

I had given Laddie Boy Reiki and talked to him mentally for hours the night before. That night, Laddie Boy lay next to me as I petted him and talked with him. Precious Pup lay at my feet the whole time. My Rock Angel Jessica knew I would have to put him to sleep the very next day, but she just couldn't bring herself to tell me. I had said, "Laddie Boy, if I have to have you put to sleep tomorrow, I want you to come to me and let me know you are okay. Just like the little doggie spirits you always knew were in the house during readings."

That very day that I had Laddie Boy put to sleep, as I was sleeping, I saw our Laddie Boy on a paved road. There were trees on either side of the road. It reminded me of the Rainbow Bridge Poem.

The Rainbow Bridge

By the edge of a woods, at the foot of a hill,
Is a lush, green meadow where time stands still.
Where the friends of man and woman do run,
When their time on earth is over and done.
For here, between this world and the next,
Is a place where each beloved creature finds rest.
On this golden land, they wait and they play,
Till the Rainbow Bridge they cross over one day.
No more do they suffer, in pain or in sadness,
For here they are whole, their lives filled with gladness.
Their limbs are restored, their health renewed,
Their bodies have healed, with strength imbued.
They romp through the grass, without even a care,
Until one day they stop, and sniff at the air.
All ears prick forward, eyes dart front and back,
Then all of a sudden, one breaks from the pack.
For just at that instant, their eyes have met;
Together again, both person and pet.
So they run to each other, these friends from long past,
The time of their parting is over at last.
The sadness they felt while they were apart,
Has turned into joy once more in each heart.
They embrace with a love that will last forever,
And then, side-by-side, they cross over...together.

Author Unknown

Pet Orbs

Once, I had taken a picture of my daughter and son-in-law at Christmas time and one of my teacher's sons looked at it. He is a very psychic young boy whom was only six years old at the time. I thought the picture had orbs in it but was not certain. The young boy had no personal knowledge of my grand dogs or that they had passed over but he saw their spirits standing behind my daughter and son-in-law and described them accurately.

Mandy My Mini-Assistant

andy, my assistant's little white dog, would meet me at my car and stayed very close to me when I would go to my assistant's house. In fact, Mandy was in most of the pictures taken at the group readings there. Mandy had many of the same mannerisms as our little dog Laddie Boy. I feel very strongly now that this is the little dog Medium/Animal Communicator Shelley Duffy tells me about in a reading which I describe later in more detail.

One day she was at my assistant's mother's house all day. There is a path through the woods from one house to the other. I told my assistant, "Mandy met me at the car." My assistant said, "That is strange. She has been at my mother's house all day until now. She must have known you were here."

During one reading, Mandy came over to me in the middle of a reading. She put her front paws up on my knees and stared me in the eyes. I said, "Okay Mandy, let me finish this reading. She wouldn't move until I had finished that part of the reading and brought through pet spirit loved ones.

Another time, while my assistant was styling my hair before readings were to start, I see this big rabbit in spirit. This rabbit was almost as big as Mandy and it was lying down beside her. I describe this rabbit to the one I am giving the reading to and she said, "Yes." She then validated the rabbit was her mother's and how no one could believe how big the rabbit had gotten.

Later, I had gone to my assistant's house when she told me how ill Mandy had become. I sat on the floor with my back straight. Mandy came over to me and she just sat in front of me. I did a rising of my energy levels with my chakras, I had my Master Guide, Guides, and Reiki Guides with me. I gave Mandy Reiki. I also talked to her mentally and introduced her to Laddie Boy. I had asked Laddie Boy to come. I said to Laddie Boy, "I want you to come and help Mandy when it comes time."

Later on in time, I had several dreams in one week. In one of the dreams, I see Laddie Boy standing next to a little white dog. I could only see the back part of the body in the dream. I never got to see the face part in the dream. My thought was, "Oh Laddie Boy is helping a little doggie."

That same week, I had another dream and Laddie was there again. Laddie Boy was sitting beside a little doggie that had been struck by a car. Again, I did not see the face. I woke up and thought, "I wonder if that is Mandy in my dreams?" I had forgotten all about these dreams when I went to my assistant's house. She told me Mandy was missing. She then goes on to tell me about a Peacock. This Peacock had come right up to the window of her house and got up onto the chair and looked in the window. Mandy did the same thing when she wanted to come into the house.

My assistant and I looked all over for Mandy. I tried psychically to pick up on where Mandy had gone. I did not think Mandy was still alive. I saw her but she wasn't moving. When I got home I called Medium/Animal Communicator, Shelley Duffy. I asked Shelley to please help me with this. I told her, "I don't want to tell my assistant that her doggie is dead and have it show up alive in time." Shelley picked up the same as I did; that Mandy was dead. She also said "we would not find Mandy's body."

I told Shelley Duffy about the Peacock. Shelley asked the same question as I did, "I wonder what Peacock means in Shamanism?" Shamanism has to do with Animal Guides. I looked it up and Peacock represents The Messenger, Death, and Resurrection.

I had another dream about Mandy a short time later. I had asked to be shown where Mandy was in a dream. In the dream, I saw a road. It was a long ways from Mandy's home. On the side of the road lay Mandy's body. I doubted what I had seen because it was too far from where Mandy lived. I never did make sense of this dream. Months later my assistant, two young adults, and I were driving down this back road where I had seen Mandy's body in my dream. I saw her body in spirit form. I knew it was her spirit body because no one else in the car saw Mandy's body. I wanted to tell my assistant to turn around and let's go back but I didn't.

We were having Group Readings for the Young Adult Group "Unity." So, I let it go and came to terms with the fact Mandy was dead. Mandy comes to both my assistant and her daughter in dreams. They often feel her spirit around them. Mandy also told my assistant's daughter in a dream that she had another doggie for them. They later got another doggie that has a lot of Mandy's mannerisms. We call him Mandy's Choice.

ALISON BAUGHMAN

I had been to Alison's website several times. Once was because well known Psychic Medium Chuck Bergman was doing an event there. I also had her site address on my website. She was a friend of two of my online teachers, Featherwind and Petz. My niece had gotten a reading from Alison at one of her chat events. I never could figure out how you could do a medium reading with numbers. Well I was in for one of the biggest surprises along my journey.

I had just started using the nickname SoulLight. As I stated earlier on in this book, often for privacy we all used chat room nick names. I was trying to move away from the nickname PrissySissy that I had used for quite a few years.

I signed in to an event, where Alison was guest speaker, with the nickname SoulLight. At the end of Alison's chat event she would be giving number readings. I had sent the question that went like this, "Why did I come back here?" I then rephrased it as, "What is my destiny?" There was no guarantee I would get a reading. I was happy when she chose me for the next reading. I could not believe the reading I received from the numbers.

In the reading, Alison gave details of my past, present, and future life. Alison then says, SoulLight your nickname speaks for itself. She says, "The last year has been the hardest year of your life. As soon as Alison said that, I just burst into tears. She was so accurate.

That was it! I decided I just had my last downward spiral and was not giving up the psychic medium study or the professional readings. I had much love and support behind the scenes.

Someone had just sent out emails to everyone around the spiritual circles of how a certified medium told him, "I was a fake, a want-to-be medium, and that I had illusions of grandeur." Well this well known professional here isn't saying that.

I continued to read her reading to me in the chat room through the tears. Alison told me, "You are very psychic." Alison goes on to tell me, "You have done this before in many lifetimes. Every hardship and experience that you had and are having in this life is to prepare you for the future." Alison goes on to say, "You are clairvoyant and clairaudient." What she meant by this is that I can see spirit and hear spirit. She said, "You have come back in this lifetime to teach. "You will teach what you have learned in this life's path."

My heart was filled with tears and I let all of them out. The tears were for healing. They were also tears of gratitude as well. Many of those people from the spiritual circle that had been sent the degrading email of me being a fake, a want-to-be medium, and which said I had illusions of grandeur were in the chat event this night.

I emailed Alison and asked her if I could return the

reading. Alison emailed back saying, "Yes, I would accept a reading from you. In return, I would like to give you a full Number Life Chart Reading."

I failed the reading I gave Alison. When it came time for the reading for Alison, I had worked all night. When I got home I couldn't sleep before the reading. I was so intimidated by this well known professional.

It was quite awhile in the future, before I worked more on confidence. At this time, I hadn't regained my confidence. I had the desire and intent to move forward in my studies and practicing the psychic medium awareness but I needed to work on restoring my confidence.

This woman Alison went on to read for me for about two hours. This was when I found out numerology readings are channeled. I didn't know this. I couldn't figure out why this beautiful gifted lady was going through all this to give me a reading. This reading was way like unbelievable.

It wasn't until much later on in my journey that I found out Alison had also studied the psychic medium awareness. She was also a Reiki Master and had studied so much more in this area. Alison's passion though is the numerology readings. My passion was to be a psychic medium.

What fascinated me so much was Alison had told me that I had been a psychic medium, in many past lifetimes. Early on in my studies of Spiritualism and in becoming a Psychic Medium, I had a dream. I was searching for answers at the time. I had asked my guides to please tell me what was happening to me. What was I and what is happening to me? Am I crazy or what? Is this the devil's work?" I had asked, "Please let the information be brought to me in dreams." I often didn't believe what I was picking up in waking hours. In this dream I heard a God like voice tell me, "You were a Psychic Medium Detective in another lifetime. You were afraid of your gifts. You wouldn't use your gifts before to help others." Well that was in the beginning of my studies. I hadn't even given readings to others yet. I just thought it was a dream. Just like with Psychic Medium Chuck Bergman, I didn't believe the dream either.

Alison continued on telling me how I was psychic and clairvoyant. She told me how very clairsentient I am and exactly what this meant. You are empath, empath, empath and you soak up energies of others like a sponge. She told me and validated to me everything I had figured out this past year.

I was psychic and could even hear others thoughts of me at times. I soaked up others energies like a sponge and would become just like them. I wasn't protecting myself enough and still don't at times. I am more aware of it now when it happens. I get my act together and do all that is necessary to remove the energies of others around me and those left from readings.

In her reading, Alison also explained what each number meant. She was spot on. Accurate in all she said. She explained what my missing numbers are and what they meant. Now I knew more about what I needed to change and work on. It is true what you hear, "The numbers do not lie." Alison had just given me a reading of a lifetime. The reading from Alison has had a profound effect on me ever since. When someone comes along who tries to degrade me, in no way do I allow it.

Alison Baughman to this day is such an inspiration in my life. Alison like all the other professionals in my life is much more than just a professional. They are all beautiful souls. They have all become like family to me. They are not smug or ego based. Alison is one of the best friends any human being could ever have.

MY STEP DAD

My mother had known my step dad for most of her life. Mom had become a widow several years before. I will call my step dad "Pa" in this story. Most of us did anyway. I will refer to my mother as "Ma" in this chapter because that is what I call her. Pa was divorced. One time or another, he would be there for all of us, in some way. Pa helped Ma save my life when I took a drug overdose while trying to commit suicide. I had been out on a wild drunk. My entire life was out of control. I had been out looking for love in all the wrong places again.

Everyone was tired of my out of control drinking. I had arguments with quite a few people around me. My own daughter wasn't even talking to me at the time. The night I tried to commit suicide, I had had an argument with the man I was dating. I didn't think I would be hurting anyone but myself. As time goes on in my study of the psychic medium awareness, I learn what committing suicide does to the ones left behind.

Pa was raised Catholic. Pa said, "Helen you need to put

her away, so she doesn't kill herself." Pa loved me I know. He was only concerned for me.

He tried to teach us the best he could. He definitely had a handful with all of us. It was the only grandpa many of the children knew. Pa and Ma raised my daughter for me. I was too busy getting drunk. I guess you could say I was out trying to find myself. I ended up back home with Ma and Pa quite a few times myself. I just couldn't make it on my own. I had limited education due to my own fault. I just couldn't afford to live on my own.

Finally, I moved out and had been living alone for quite awhile. Ma and Pa still looked after me though. I would go to their house and Ma would cook breakfast for us. When Precious Pup and Laddie Boy were with me, Laddie Boy ended up in Pa's lap and Precious Pup was in the kitchen watching Ma cook breakfast for she knew Ma would cook her an egg. Of course Laddie Boy got fed as well.

As usual, we played some cards. Ma and Pa drank very heavy at one time. After Pa's last drunk driving offense, he attended Alcoholics Anonymous Meetings. Ma would drive him to the meetings. After that, they both quit drinking. They both had close to thirty years of sobriety.

Pa had also quit smoking for two years. I used to wonder if Pa's depression stemmed from his quitting smoking. I use to say, "Pa, if you want I will go down to the store and buy you a pack of cigarettes. You can have some of my cigarettes if you'd like." He would always say, "No, not today." Pa complained about chronic pain in his back. He was back and forth to the doctors and hospital. Mom was back and forth to the doctors and hospital with her health problems. There at the last few months it was one or the other of them going every few days.

Pa was in the hospital getting ready to have kidney stone surgery. Now I had seen my son-in-law go through this. How painful it was. While he was waiting to go downstairs for surgery, I was sitting there reading a book about one of the most famous mediums on television. Pa asked, "What are you reading?" Pa and Ma were playing a game of cards. I started to laugh about what the famous medium had experienced. Pa always loved a good joke. I started reading some paragraphs out of the book to Pa.

Pa, Ma, and I talked many days about the psychic medium awareness and what I was experiencing at the time. Often times, after my brother was locked up in prison, Pa and I would talk about it, I would say, "Don't worry about it Pa because we have Heaven On Our Side. We just have to Believe In It and It Will Take Us There!

I tried to bring through a reading to Pa from his brother who had passed. Ma told me not to talk about it so I stopped. Pa's brother was laughing because we were arguing over the card game. I could see him on the Heaven level just laughing at us. He was right; we were like a bunch of kids when we played cards.

Pa was in the emergency room and one of my brothers was there. I was showing this same book to him telling him what the famous medium could do. He looks at the doctor and jokingly said, "I think you have the wrong person in that bed. I think you need to take him off the bed and admit her." It hurt Pa to laugh but he still laughed. He always had that good sense of humor.

For some reason, I had said to Ma and Pa when Pa was going for his kidney stone surgery, "Let's make a pact" and I held the book up, "Whenever we go, whoever goes first, we will send a message to the others from the other side."

Pa and Ma knew that I meant that whoever passes first and crosses will send a message to the others letting them know that person has arrived and/or that he/she is okay.

I went to the hospital to see Pa after the surgery several days later. They were sending him home that day when I went to see him. Pa was in so much pain he begged the doctors not to send him home. Along with the chronic pain he had in his back for the last two years, there was this pain added to it. He literally begged them not to send him home like that.

I walked outside with my step sister, Pa's daughter. I went off. I said, "You get your husband on the phone. Find a way to get him up the road to a hospital that would help him get rid of the pain. Maybe the doctors up the road can find out what is causing the pain." "They are sending him home in all that pain." I had lost it. I broke down so bad. I told them they needed to get him somewhere. That wasn't the first time I broke bad on someone over this. I broke bad on my family doctor as we all shared the same doctor. I said, "If you can't find out what is wrong with him then let us know. We will find someone who can." I was embarrassed at my actions as I saw the look on our doctor's face. I just couldn't stand seeing Pa in pain like that.

I had picked Ma up at the hospital and took her home. She had been back in there also. Pa said, "Stay and we will play a game of cards." I said, "I will on my next day off, Pa. I have to sleep a couple hours before I go to work tonight."

It wasn't too many days later, I was sleeping and I heard the phone recorder kick in. It was my brother calling to say he was taking our mom back to the hospital. She wouldn't go in the ambulance so Pa had called my brother to go take her. My brother had called Pa's daughter up out of concern and asked her to go pick Pa up so he would not be home alone. He also told her that we were with our mom at the hospital. I went to meet my mother and brother at the emergency room. I later tried to call Pa to let him know that mom had taken a test and we were waiting for the results but he didn't answer the phone. I guess this was in the neighborhood of three or three-thirty p.m. EST. I figured he had gone to stay with his daughter at that point. After awhile, my brother said, "Since you are here, I am going home and try to catch a couple hours of sleep." I said, "Okay, I will stay here with Ma."

It didn't seem like too many hours had went by when my brother's wife came in with my nephew. I was surprised to see her there. I thought it was awful late for her to be out when their son had school the next day. She says, "Glenda your daughter needs you." I said, "I can't leave Ma." She said it again persistently, "Glenda your daughter needs you and you need to go to her." My daughter's father had just been diagnosed with terminal cancer about a week prior. My mother said, "Go to your daughter, she needs you." My brother's wife said, "I will stay here until you come back." Ma looked so bad that I didn't want to leave her.

My sister-in-law and I had walked outside. I didn't know if I should go or not. My sister-in-law asked, "Glenda, do you want me to tell you why you need to go?" I looked directly at her now. The look on her face told me it was not good. I just wasn't for sure what. I said, "No, Don't tell me because I don't want to have a problem driving there. I will just wait to find out when I get there." I knew I needed to go and my sister-in-law was staying with Ma so I went.

When I got there, both my brother and my daughter were crying uncontrollably. My daughter's mother-in-law and father-in-law were there also. My son-in-law was out of town on business. My brother and daughter through the tears look at me and asked, "You know, don't you?" I asked, "Know what?" They both acted as though they didn't want to tell me. I asked again, "Know what?" They thought my sister-in-law had told me.

As they thought I would, I was thinking my daughter's father had passed. I was getting a little frantic but held it in control for my daughter's sake. My brother was very close to my daughter's father also and this is why I was thinking he was crying uncontrollably. Finally, my brother came out and said "Pa shot himself." I screamed, "NOOOOOO he can't do this to us, Oh, my dear God in Heaven NOOO." My crying was more a scream of agony. I pulled myself together some how. I didn't know how I did it at the time. I, all of a sudden just stopped crying and it was like a calm that came over me.

I realized a lot of thoughts that I thought were mine were not mine in the days that followed. I didn't know it at the time but I was being overshadowed. It took along time afterwards to piece it all together.

It dawned on me that we needed to keep this quiet from Ma. This would send her on out of this world and that we would be burying them both at the same time. To this day, I do not know if those were my thoughts or not.

The first thing we needed to do was make sure they weren't taking Pa's body to the hospital. At this time, Ma was still in the emergency room. I told my brother that we had to pull ourselves together here.

I know today that the calmness came from above. I didn't have that kind of strength. The days that followed are like being in a nightmare always hoping you wake up soon.

I think my brother left to help out with the rest of the family. I went back to the hospital and spent the night there. I believe that is the same night my brother and one of my sisters came to the hospital. We all three slept on the couch that converted into a bed.

My sister woke herself and me up talking in her sleep. I was glad she did. I had Astral Traveled down to Pa's and Ma's house. I was walking around all over yelling for Pa. I was hollering, "Why?" I said, "Pa, I know you are here somewhere and I want to know why? Why did you do this?"

My sister and I both were concerned about saying something that Ma would pick up on. We decided to stay awake the rest of the night. We knew we had to be careful.

It was getting close to the time for Pa's funeral. We had to tell Ma as soon as the doctors thought she could handle it. Everyone was working together on this. The entire hospital staff was working with us to keep this from Ma. We had the phone connection to her hospital room disconnected. We screened everyone who came in the room and reminded them not to say anything at all. Quite a few times we found her picking up the phone to call Pa. She couldn't understand why the phone didn't work in her room. We left our cell phones sitting around a few times and found Ma trying to call Pa. She wondered why Pa wasn't answering the phone. Ma also couldn't understand why Pa hadn't been there to see her yet. For our mother's health, we had been telling one lie right after another to cover up the fact that Pa was dead.

It was time to tell Ma as the funeral was approaching, so one of my brothers told Ma after the entire family was there at the hospital with her including our family from North Carolina. Pa's son and one of his daughters were there as well when we told Ma. At this point, we purposely did not tell Ma exactly how Pa had died because we didn't think she could handle it. We told her she needed to focus on her own health.

The hospital staff had set out refreshments for everyone during this time. They didn't know if Ma was going to make it through this either as she had been diagnosed with congestive heart failure along with her many other health issues. The support we received was unbelievable.

It was just before the funeral that one of my other brothers told Ma that Pa had shot himself. The doctor was there both times to give her a sedative, if needed.

When my sister who is a nurses' assistant got in town and came to the hospital, I decided to go home for a while. I went home and took care of our two doggies that were still with us at the time. I then went in and sat on the couch. I kept asking, "Why, Why, Why?" I went straight in and got on the computer. The thought had come to me to look online at the medical dictionary. I typed in the word shingles.

Ma had mentioned Pa had shingles. I had never heard of shingles before this. My sister who is the nurses' assistant had said the shingles were very painful. I looked at several sections of the medical dictionary. At first I wasn't finding what I was looking for, by then I realized Pa was with me. I was watching Laddie Boy. Whenever you spoke to Laddie Boy he would cock his head from one side to the other as though he was listening to you talk to him. Laddie Boy was looking in the air doing this. I knew that he saw Pa and that Pa was talking to him.

I continued to search the medical dictionary and then I saw what I was looking for. There it was. I read it and reread it so I could understand as much as I could. It described exactly what the shingles were and what caused them to surface again after so many years had gone by. It said that if you ever had the chicken pox it basically lay dormant. It gave you all the reasons that could activate it again. It went on to tell you how if your immune system was too weak to fight the shingles it would end up in a never ending oh so painful pain. That is how it explained it. A never ending oh so painful pain. It showed this pain being right where Pa had showed us where he was hurting. It or Pa made me understand it was like a hot poker stick in his back. That is what Pa always told us that it had a burning feeling.

I printed a few copies of all this out for the family. So they may better understand the why. I guess we never did understand, until then, exactly how much pain he was in. I then started writing what I thought was a eulogy. Everyone said I could do this best. I started to write a eulogy but ended up writing a Why, Pa did this to go with all I printed about the shingles. I realize today what I had done was not write a why from my point of view. I was writing for Pa. He was having me write his reasons for doing this. The pain had become so unbearable that none of the painkillers worked anymore. The dictionary said there was no cure for it. Pa felt the only thing left for him was go to the hospital up the road and survive by being shot up with morphine until he passed.

When I had finished writing all this, I hear Pa say to me in thought form, "I am going to the hospital to be with Ma now. I need to give her some energy." In an ozone state of mind, I said out loud, "You do that Pa. Ma is going to need all the energy that she can get." I looked up at the clock above my computer desk. It said 2:30 A.M EST. I decided to take a shower and go to bed. I decided to not go back to the hospital until I slept for a few hours.

I went back to the hospital. I had read to Ma, one of my sisters and one of my brothers all that I had printed out about the shingles. All of this seemed strange for me to do at the time. I often did strange things but later on it comes to light. I can look back and it was Spirit or the Divine Universe guiding me. Overshadowing me with their thoughts.

My sister and I had gone down to the cafeteria and got us something to eat. My brother, sister, Ma, and I were eating. I was taking a bite of my food when Ma said, "I saw my Pa last night. It was around 2:30 in the morning. I had to get up and go to the bathroom. All I could see is his face and it looked shadowy, but I knew it was my Pa coming to see me." She looked sad all of a sudden and said, "Or maybe it was my imagination."

I started choking on my food and almost dropped my whole plate of food. I remembered that was the exact time Pa had told me that he was going to the hospital to see Ma. I remembered looking up at the clock above my computer desk. Pa kept his word and Ma made it through the funeral.

Ironically, many years later, as I finish writing this book, my mother has developed shingles and it is a haunting reminder to her and agonizing pain for her in many ways.

*What haunted me was the man who helped save my life from attempted suicide eventually committed suicide.

Medium/Animal Communicator, Shelley Duffy

It wasn't long after Pa committed suicide that I had many questions about suicide. I went and read all I could on it. The first place I looked was in some of the books I had that the famous medium had written.

I went to the famous medium's resource page. I knew from experience just going through the list a few times I would know whom to call. I studied her picture for a long time. I had the feeling she was the medium I needed to contact. I couldn't explain why but she had the gentlest energies. I don't think at the time I was actually doing a psychic reading connection here with the picture of Shelley Duffy. Maybe I was.

I contacted Shelley Duffy. I got an appointment within a few weeks. I called my sister-in-law and invited her and her mother. They came over and they were on the other phone. We tried to tape the session but my recorder was one of the older models and didn't record well at all. In the beginning, I hadn't said anything at all about myself being able to communicate with spirit. However, it was coming out later on in the reading. Still at this time, I didn't know much at all about my gifts and hadn't yet taken the online practice reading classes.

I thought maybe I would call Shelley a few minutes early. The thought came; no she wouldn't be ready yet. She is precise on her times. I realize today spirit was telling me this.

Shelley's reading goes as follow: She describes my step dad perfectly. She goes on and tells how he was when here. What she was actually doing was telling me word for word the eulogy I had written. I had lost three or four pages of the eulogy. Shelley even brought through what I had written on the pages that I had lost. Shelly said, "Someone at the funeral dressed in blue wrote something about him." My sister-in-law said my niece ALA was dressed in blue. I didn't remember that. She says Pa says there wasn't a dry eye in the place when I read what she had written. I recalled everyone sobbing when I was reading the poem ALA had written.

ALA had told me that she felt a feathery feeling on her hand like a brush on her hand when I was reading what she wrote. I said, "That is Pa letting you know he is here with us." This to me validated what I had said to ALA. It also validated to me that spirit is at their funeral. I said, "Yes Shelley you are correct. I read a poem that my niece, his granddaughter had written for him. I remember everyone there burst in tears and you could hear the sobbing." Shelley said, "This is strange, he says he has it with him. He is talking about having something with him." I said, "No Shelley it is not strange. Before they closed the casket ALA and I walked up to it, and I said okay ALA put your poem in there with Pa." ALA asked, "Where should I put it? Should

I put it on the side?" I said, "No ALA you wrote it from your heart so you should lay it across his heart." She did: She laid the poem across his heart. Pa had even told Shelley that many were there at his prayer service that he never even thought would come. She then gave me the names. Ma had told me about them being there. My brother's widow was there with her current husband. Pa was very surprised and pleased about that.

There was no way Shelley could have known this because I had never mentioned it in any of the chats or anything. I asked Shelley, "Can you ask Pa if there is anyone else around him?" Shelley said, "He said this was his forum and he wasn't finished talking yet. He was like this in his life here." I said. "Yes, he was." Pa talked about a lot. Shelley gave detailed accurate information. Shelley told us exactly what his son-in-law had gotten up and said at the funeral mass. Later, he gave the floor so to speak to other family members.

She brought through my biological father and described everything about his passing and about the argument before. Ma and my biological father had an argument just prior to his passing. Shelley couldn't have known that. I never talked about that in or around any of the chat rooms.

She then brought through many of my sister-in-law's family. My sister-in-law is better at

picking up on things during a reading than I am. This happened a lot during the reading with Shelley. Shelley described a man that was helping Pa crossover to the other side. I wasn't picking up on exactly who it was but I had several people in mind. My sister-in-law knew exactly who it was though. She said, "Haven't you ever seen the picture at your mother's house?" The man Shelley was describing was father to one of my nephew's. The nephew's father had also shot himself. I again tell you I don't have all the answers. The psychic medium awareness is a forever learning process. I do feel the fact that my nephew's father had shot himself and Pa had shot himself played a part in my nephew's father helping Pa to crossover. It was like they shared a connection that only they could understand. Perhaps in time, on my journey, I will learn more answers about this.

Pa told Shelley he was hanging around until everyone goes home. He was talking about everyone who was here from out of State. Pa loved family gatherings. He loved Ma's North Carolina Family.

You may recall me mentioning earlier, that I would tell you in more detail later about a reading Shelley gave me involving a little white dog. In this reading, Shelley also talked about how spirit told her some things before even calling me; she heard this lady has communication with spirit abilities. She then tells me about a little dog that will be helping me tune in the gifts of the psychic medium awareness. Shelley kept talking about a white dog. She says the dog was here. Mandy is the white dog you see in all the pictures of my readings on my website. She was my assistant's little dog as said earlier.

Shelley had brought so many spirit loved ones through that day. Everything Shelley said was detailed and accurate. No one could have known many of the details that she brought through for they were never talked about.

When Pa committed suicide, I was in such shock. With suicide being so taboo and my lack of knowledge on the subject at the time, I really didn't like talking about it and I didn't. Shelley assured me Pa had crossed over. All would be fine. Pa receives spiritual help on the other side. That is why

I feel my nephew's father came and helped him crossover. Pa saw when he got to Heaven those he hurt and left behind.

In the beginning of the reading from Shelley, Pa kept talking about coughing and lungs and insisted it was me he was talking about Shelley said. This part of the reading went on for awhile. I said, "No Shelley my mom has COPD."COPD is a lung disease caused from smoking. Shelley said, "Glenda, He said you have it." I insisted he was talking about mom. Shelley stood by what she was hearing. A year later, I find out I do have COPD just like my mom.

Remember earlier in this book, months before Pa's passing, I had a precognitive dream. In the dream, my mom was over across the bridge at a house. It was during a bad storm. I couldn't understand whose house she was at. I couldn't understand why Pa wasn't with her. I kept wondering where Pa was when I woke up from the dream. Now we know why Pa wasn't with Ma. Find out how this comes to light, in the days that followed this dream.

My journey in the Psychic Medium Awareness is a continued learning experience. I cannot tell it all in one book. Spirit told me long ago that I would write three books. Spirit was correct even though I did not believe it at the time. Join me in my next book.

A Lost Soul

I was a lost soul. Through my life I became bitter, thinking life cheated me and dealt me a bad hand. I hated everything and a lot of people. I had been married and divorced three times. I looked for love in all the wrong places. I thought if men thought I was attractive and they wanted to date me, they cared about me. I needed to be wanted to feel any self-worth. All my life I wanted outside approval to feel like I was someone and worth something. I hated God. Eventually, I just didn't believe in him at all. I felt that no God would have taken my father from us, especially when he was only forty-three years old. This had left my mother with three young boys to raise alone. When my brother Joe was killed in a car accident, it was the last straw between me and any God.

I became the same thing that I hated in my father when he was an alcoholic. That was until I became a recovering alcoholic. I then went back to school and got my diploma. Yet I was still missing something. I was afraid of everything and everybody. I had so much fear in me. I was afraid of living, dying, driving a car, and trusted no one. I felt worthless and that my life was no better than when I stayed drunk. I had searched the world over for answers. I questioned what life was about and what it was for. It wasn't until I went to see the famous medium that the answers would eventually come.

Finding Myself

When I started doing the spirit communications, I realized that our loved ones never leave us. They don't die. Even our pet loved ones live on. I even said to myself early on, "Wow, it is like they never left us."

During the readings, when I would bring through the ones who drank and did drugs, it showed me what it did to the ones left behind. It showed me what I had done to my family, friends and others.

Bringing through ones who committed suicide showed me what my trying to commit suicide did to my loved ones. I thought I wasn't hurting anyone but myself. Those that did commit suicide showed me the pain and how it affected others.

Doing the meditations and learning more on the psychic medium awareness, I also learned that I was a spiritual being in a human body. I learned all I needed to do was go within and tap into the spiritual being I am.

My looking for love in all the wrong places and people, I learned I had to be the love I wanted to receive. I found I attracted people to me just like I was. Today, I now know that I don't have to look to others or outside myself to find love. As for my hating others, I learned I needed to forgive them for they are on their own path and journey. I also needed to forgive myself for all the mistakes I made and things I did that I felt were wrong for it was only then that I could move on spiritually.

ALL THAT I CAN BE

After finding out who I really am, a spiritual being, and not the worthless person who never did anything good, I had to learn to like me again. Then, I had to love myself in order to truly love others.

I realized that I had not done anything constructive with my life. I don't ever remember me helping others to any degree or worth. It was always about me. I have learned to care about others and their pain and suffering. I now want to help others, like I have been helped. I want to try to help others realize the spiritual being they are and help them to know they can be all they want to be.

I found the God that I lost or left behind so many years ago. I have even become an ordained Reverend. I do believe in God and all man kinds higher good.

For several years I was attuned to be a Reiki One Healer. Reiki is a type of alternative healing. You can google this type of healing or read resource books to find out more about Reiki. It is using the Divine Source, energies, and your own healing power from within. I decided to move forward in this type of healing and became a Reiki Master Teacher.

In learning the Psychic Medium Awareness, I found out who I really am and all I can become. In my journey I wish to help others with my experiences, strength, hope, and healing.

Heaven Is Ours!
Against All Odds!

Against all odds, I continued to study the psychic medium awareness no matter the obstacles and/or challenges. I knew I wanted to reach out and help others the way I had been helped. I want the town where I live to become more open and be aware of the powers of one within. I want to mostly reach out to the younger generation. Teach them that they don't have to be fifty years old like me to learn the gifts they have within them. I want them to know there is no peer pressure, they all are leaders, and can change our world to be a better place. The young generations of today are the world's future. I want them to learn like I learned that alcohol and or drugs are not the answers.

The psychic medium awareness is not taught in the schools or the alcohol and drug rehabilitation centers. I wanted to go public to show others who don't know, that it can be done. We all have the psychic ability and can use it to better our lives on a daily basis. This is what I teach before and after my readings.

I first started this with the younger generation at work. We would get together during our lunch hour and I would do readings.

I had gone public already. I put an advertisement in the local newspaper. I put my first name, my website address, and my phone number on the advertisement. I had put a picture of me from 1992 hoping no one would recognize me. I went to four different government offices to get my business permit before getting to the right office. One young woman looked at me and I read her thoughts. She was thinking, "You don't look like a psychic." I thought back to her with a smile, "What is a psychic supposed to look like?" I did get my permit.

Heaven Is Ours! Is the name spirit gave me for my business. Spirit also gave me that title for my second book. I continued to give the practice readings at work. It really wasn't until I continued to do the professional in person readings that the word spread fast.

I still had unresolved issues involving family and friends who were against this. The Psychic Medium Awareness was taboo. Against all odds, I was finally feeling like I was making progress. Slowly others could see I was serious and I was doing what I said I could do." Heaven Is Ours! Against All Odds! Also means I have a loving God no matter my past as long as I grow spiritually and believe in God I will also go to Heaven. In my book "Heaven Is Ours! Against All Odds!" I pick up where I leave off in this book.

THE LIGHTHOUSE MEMORIES

The lighthouse stands strong against the winds,
From the beginning till the end
The lighthouses' beacon of light shines forever in the
night,
The beacon of light burning so bright

The beam of light carries us through the foggy days,
The beam of light carries us through our lonely nights
The beam of light carries us through our life

Our loved ones are like that
The lighthouse beam of light,
That forever burns so bright in memories
There they leave it in our hearts, mind, soul, and body

The love they give us, the lessons we learn
The lighthouse memories forever to be
Always the light of their heart and soul to let us know they
are there
Even when they are passed over, we know they still care

The love and strength and guidance they still share
Their beam of light still shining bright
Forever walks with us while we are still here on earth
In our lives from day to day
In love and strength in every way

Wherever you go,
In the things you do and say
The light house memories are still there,
No one can take them away

Know that their beam of light from the Heaven and stars
Will forever be with you in every way
Shining brightly on your pathway of life,
Through the foggy days and the lonely nights

You will see the light in a song you hear,
In words of others, in special meaning phrases, in pictures,
from others love
The light will shine from above
And the light house of memories
Will forever be …

*This poem was channeled from spirit above, so I left it the
way I heard it.

*If this book can help one person to become all they can be, then I have achieved my goal.

SPECIAL ACKNOWLEDGEMENTS

I would like to give special acknowledgements to my mother, my editor, my daughter, son-in-law, grandson, brothers and sisters, step-brother and step-sisters, Barbara aka Bjean, Karen, Duane, Taylor, Chris, Dorothy, Phil, Taylor E., Julie-Anne C., Maja, Goran, Duki, Dora Crow, Shakira the cat, The Reverend, Lynda Fishman, Julie D. Hemal Radia, and Don G.

My love and gratitude goes out to the one that edited my book for me. I will be forever grateful to her. Although she has a college degree, it is not in English and she has never edited a book before now. She wishes to remain anonymous as many others chose to do with their nicknames or no names at all in this book.

My editor in her spare time from work, family, and her own life, edited my book to the best of her ability. With my limited education, I had no idea where to begin. I myself could not hire a ghostwriter. Hopefully, in the next books that spirit told me that I am going to write, they will provide the ghostwriter for me.

I wish to thank my editor's family, including their two little dogs, for they allowed her the time spent with me that could have been spent with them. My editor took the time and patience with me to try to clearly understand my experiences. Sometimes I would have to repeat several times, what I was actually feeling, hearing, and seeing during these experiences. This was so she could try to understand exactly what my experiences were like, to properly convey them, since she was not a psychic medium.

I would like to give love and gratitude to Mary Beth Weber and Asker. Without Mary Beth, this book would not have been published.

*When this book was finished my editor said when you finish writing your next book, you need to find a Ghost Editor. I asked, "Do you mean a Ghost Writer?" She said, "No a Ghost Editor!"

Sites

www.vanpraagh.com
www.michaeltamura.com
www.chuckbergman.com
www.icspirits.com
www.visiblebynumbers.com
www.joannegerber.com
www.crossingover2.com
www.kjmasters.com
www.thesmilingsoul.com
www.healgriefwithbelief.com
www.repairingrainbows.com
www.bbsradio.com
www.edgarcayce.org
www.shrineofhope.com
www.johnedward.net
www.daniellemackinnon.com
www.TheSpiritArtist.com
www.gethisnumber.com

Books

James Van Praaghs' Books

You Are The Answer – Michael Tamura

Evidence of the Afterlife-
Joseph Higgins & Chuck Bergman

Repairing Rainbows-Lynda Fishman

I Can Do It – Louise Hay

Over The Rainbow Bridge –
Shirley Enebrad

Get His Number – Alison Baughman

John Holland's Books

John Edward's Books

There Is A River – Edgar Cayce Books

Echo Bodine's Books

Never Letting Go - Mark Anthony

These books can be found on the sites mentioned above. I found most, if not all, of the books on www.amazon.com.

About the Author

My name is Glenda Ann Abell. I was born in Fort Bragg, North Carolina. I was raised in Southern Maryland. I am fifty-seven years old and the third oldest of twelve children. I have been married and divorced three times. I am a mother of one, mother-in-law, and grandmother to a wonderful grandson and two grand dogs. I am a recovering alcoholic. I quit school in ninth grade and returned at the age of thirty-eight to receive my high school diploma. I took a basic course in typing. Everything I learned on the computer was by trial and error.

In 2005, my whole world changed when I went to see a world renowned famous medium in Virginia. I was fifty-one years old and had looked for love in all the wrong places my entire life. I was bitter, cold hearted, and I hated my life.

I had been sober for about thirteen years. I was missing something in my life. I had no self esteem, felt I had not accomplished anything in my life. I had no self worth at all. I hated God and eventually had no faith at all.

Join me in my journey through the psychic medium awareness where I found all the above. It can be done, no matter your past or present. Find out how I searched the world over for answers that I never found until I went to see World-Renowned Medium James Van Praagh!